Exporting from Canada

Exporting from Canada

Gerhard W. Kautz

Self-Counsel Press
(a division of)
International Self-Counsel Press Ltd.
Canada   USA

Self-Counsel Press acknowledges the financial support of the Government of Canada through the Book Publishing Industry Development Program (BPIDP) for our publishing activities.

Printed in Canada.

First edition: 2002

National Library of Canada Cataloguing in Publication Data

Kautz, Gerhard, 1938-
   Exporting from Canada

(Self-counsel business series)
1-55180-342-9

1. Exporting marketing—Canada. I. Title. II. Series.
HF1416.6.C3K38 2002   658.8'48   C2002-910762-8

Self-Counsel Press Inc.
(a division of)
International Self-Counsel Press Ltd.

1481 Charlotte Road	1704 N. State Street
North Vancouver, BC V7J 1H1	Bellingham, WA 98225
Canada	USA

CONTENTS

INTRODUCTION

This book is aimed primarily at small- and medium-size Canadian companies that are considering the export market. It can also be used as a basic training manual for those new to exporting. It covers the major aspects of entering the international market, from the initial decision to export, through the various activities required, such as identifying a suitable market and establishing an agent or local representative in a foreign country, to eventually signing a sales contract, shipping, and receiving payment. The book deals with the practical issues of exporting, based on the experience of the author, who has done business in more than 40 countries over the past 20 years.

Anecdotes of problems and situation arising from international trade activity are provided throughout the book to illustrate the points made. These examples are based on actual events, but the names and sometimes places have been changed.

In addition to detailing how to make a first entry into the international market, the book offers information about contacts that can provide additional information and assist your exporting initiative. These contacts range from federal and provincial government departments to organizations such as banks and trade associations. Information is also provided on specific government export assistance programs. In order for the reader to keep this information up to date, throughout the book you will find many references to the Internet and the large number of useful Web sites available. Unfortunately some Web sites, particularly government sites, may have changed since this book was written, but you should find sufficient information here to locate the new addresses.

To help you make your exporting initiative more efficient, checklists are included to help you with the following exporting tasks —

- to help you better understand and plan exporting costs,
- to clarify which legal issues you must contend with,
- to meet the basic requirements for a business trip abroad, and
- to help you remember and meet all of the deadlines involved in exhibiting at trade shows in the export market.

Detailed information is provided in appendices on —

- NAFTA-qualifying professions for cross-border travel and work,
- locations of both federal and provincial government export assistance offices,
- a list of trade and industry organizations offering export assistance, and
- an explanation of how the carnet system works.

The following conventions are used in the book in the interest of brevity, and no other meaning should be read into them:

- The term "product" refers to both goods and services, unless otherwise specified.
- The term "agent" refers to an individual or company that acts as a representative of foreign suppliers. The use of the masculine when referring to an agent or agency is not meant to offend but to reflect the reality of the predominance of men in this field.

1
TO EXPORT OR
NOT TO EXPORT

This chapter introduces the issues associated with exporting your products. It is intended to help you determine whether or not you should enter the export market. The discussion continues in more detail in following chapters.

1. Why Export?

Canada is an exporting nation. Exports are the main reason Canada's relatively small population is able to enjoy a high standard of living. Most medium- and large-size Canadian companies consider exporting a natural part of their business, as do many smaller businesses. If your company is not exporting its products, you should consider this additional market opportunity.

The major reason to begin exporting is to increase sales. This is particularly true if you have a niche market product and you have sold as many as you think can possibly be sold in the domestic market (you have saturated the domestic market). Assuming that your domestic sales cover your fixed costs, you can develop export sales that will provide a higher profit for you. The extra sales volume and profit that export sales provide may then allow you to reduce your cost of production and your prices and so gain more of the domestic market share from your competitors.

Another reason to enter the international market is to diversify your customer base and counter the effects of a slowdown in your domestic market. For example, in the late 1990s the US economy was booming but Canadian markets were taking longer to heat up. Companies that were exporting to the United States fared much better than their counterparts who concentrated on only the Canadian market.

Do not consider the export market as a cure for an ailing company, however. If you have cash-flow or other financial problems now, attempting the export market will only make the situation worse. Getting into the export market is going to cost you a lot of money, and it could be a few years before you make your first sale. If you do not have the finances to do the job right, perhaps you should first focus on improving your domestic business.

2. Which Products Can You Export?

When considering exporting, the first question you have to answer is, "Do you have an exportable product?" Some companies must answer this basic question with "No," or "No, unless we change it." For example. if you have software or processes that could be adapted to other languages such as Spanish or Arabic, you may find customers in Latin America or the Middle East.

Another problem that many small companies have is that their products were specially designed for a particular customer, and are not suitable for other customers. For example, you may provide services translating government documents into French from English or from English into French. This is an almost uniquely Canadian requirement, and would not be appealing to many foreign customers. These products will have to be changed not only to appeal to foreign customers, but probably to gain other domestic sales as well. Similarly, in the process of altering the product for domestic customers, it may be useful to keep in mind the foreign market.

A third problem for small- to medium-size companies is that they have a variety of different products. Some products may serve one particular customer, yet others attract a group of customers. You must identify which products you want to emphasize in a foreign marketing effort. You don't want to make the mistake of trying to sell everything, because it will dilute your marketing thrust. Different products will appeal to different customers and will require different marketing approaches. You don't want to bite off more than your marketing budget can chew.

You must also consider which products can be exported profitably. You may have to go through such major redesign efforts and costs to make your products suitable for foreign buyers that could result in an overall loss even if you do eventually sell them overseas. The first question you must ask, therefore, is not only "Do I have an exportable product?" but also "Do I have an exportable product that I can export profitably?" The next few chapters in this book will help you answer these questions.

3. Evaluate Your Company's Track Record

Most successful exporting businesses have established a solid track record in the domestic market before turning their energies to the international scene. The local market gives them an in-depth familiarity with their product and how to market it successfully. While deciding whether or not to export and while identifying a profitable export product, you must look at your current domestic business. Are there similar customers in other countries? Will they be willing and able to pay as much as or more than your current customers? Can you use the same marketing techniques with them?

The answer to these and other related questions will give you a good indication of your export possibilities. Yet there is more to exporting than simply expanding your activity to another country. You will have to identify the desired country, look at the costs of exporting to it, consider the legal requirements, and decide on a business arrangement in the country, and that's only getting started. Other issues will arise as you begin exporting to the target country. The following chapters will provide you with guidelines for evaluating whether the increased administration of exporting to another country balances the increased sales revenue you will achieve.

4. Rethink Product Applications

A key part of identifying suitable foreign markets for a product is to consider how current customers use your product. For example, a central heating system is used in Canada to heat buildings during the cold winter weather. It obviously will not appeal to anyone in the Caribbean, but will be very desirable in the northern provinces of China and other countries that have cold winter weather. It is fairly easy to identify countries with potential customers for this product, but for most other products it is not as simple. Nevertheless, a good start in identifying new markets is to analyze how customers currently use your product.

As you analyze the existing market for your product, try to "think outside the box." Using the same example, the central heating system may also appeal to some customers in countries with very hot summers and slightly cooler winters, such as in the Middle East. Even though the winter temperature is still well above freezing, it can be uncomfortable to have unheated houses, especially at night. These people can often afford the luxury of a central heating system, and it may even be prestigious for them to have one in their home. A small but lucrative market for the heating system could exist in this hot climate.

5. Identify Possible Export Markets

If you have been thinking about exporting your products, you probably have thought of possible markets already. There may be potential customers in each of these market areas, but the trick is to target the markets with the greatest potential for profit. If you don't, you could expend a lot of time and marketing budget on a low-paying or even losing effort.

Don't be lured to a foreign market for the wrong reasons, such as a trade show that you've heard about that caters to your products. Similarly, knowing somebody with good connections in a particular country is not necessarily a good reason to seek an export market there. The granddaddy of all bad reasons is finding a market in a country that has a nice climate for a winter vacation. Decide on your potential export market logically rather than emotionally. This book will help you in this approach.

6. Gain Management Commitment

Before you begin spending your marketing funds on a foreign market, ensure that you have the management commitment to "stay the course." You may need to take quite a while to develop the market to the stage where it is profitable, or even to get the first sale, depending on your product. Make sure senior management is aware of this, and support the effort. Otherwise you may find your marketing efforts cut short by lack of funding, or worse. Exporting is a long-term company commitment that can be very profitable.

7. Additional Information

The Internet has a wealth of information on international business opportunities. The following Web sites are well worth exploring and bookmarking for future use. Additional resources are available in print.

1. Canadian government Industry Canada Strategis site for business and consumer information at <strategis.ic.gc.ca>.

2. Canadian government Department of Foreign Affairs and International Trade Infoexport site for the Canadian Trade Commissioner Service at <www.infoexport.gc.ca>.

3. *Start and Run an Exporting Business.* Laurel L. Delaney. Self-Counsel Press, 1998.

2
COSTS OF EXPORTING

This chapter takes an initial look at the costs you will face as you tackle the export market. It is not meant to scare you out of the exporting business, but rather as a forewarning of the costs that lie ahead. Depending on your product, a showstopper cost may come along that will dash your export hopes. Most costs, though, are an extension of your current costs of doing business. Others may be new to you. All are simply the price of expanding your business. The Exporting Costs List at the end of the chapter, will help you to better understand and plan your costs.

1. Marketing and Promotion Costs

Marketing and promotion costs will probably be your biggest additional cost. The increased marketing costs can be expected in three areas: personnel, travel, and promotional literature.

1.1 Cost of new personnel

The export market will require a lot of attention from your marketing staff, so you may have to hire additional people to address the new business. This can create a major expense for a small company. You can avoid some of this expense by using consultants or trading houses. (See the section on trading houses in Chapter 4, Export Business Arrangements.)

1.2 Travel costs

Your export marketing staff will have to travel to the target countries, and these trips can be very expensive. You will have to consider the cost of airfare as well as living expenses. Hotels alone can cost more than $300 per day, and meals in reasonable restaurants are usually much more expensive in foreign countries than they are in Canada. Local transportation will also add to the bill, particularly if you are travelling in a large country and the potential customers are widely spread.

1.3 Cost of new promotional literature

Your initial marketing activity in a country will probably be with local agents or importers who have a good grasp of the English language. Your existing product literature should suffice, but eventually you may have to translate your brochures, videos, and other documents into the local language. This cost can be reduced by getting your local agent to help with the translation, once you've established an agent in the country. But you will still have to foot the bill of producing the new literature.

When you estimate these marketing and promotion costs, consider the need for several visits to the target country, and the many months, if not years, before you get your first contract. You will discover as you work through this book that there is plenty of groundwork to do before you make foreign sales. This work may be expensive but, once accomplished, the effort can be quite profitable.

2. Cost of Product Redesign

The product you are currently selling to your Canadian customers may have to be changed for the foreign market. There could be a number of reasons for product redesign. Identify any changes you may have to make now rather than later when you discover additional costs you did not expect. Some of the issues you should consider at this time include the following:

♦ Will your product have to be tested and approved for regulatory or safety standards in the country you are considering? Will you have to redesign the product to meet these requirements?

♦ Will you have to modify the electrical aspects of the product? Many parts of the world operate on a 220 volt or 240 volt power supply versus the 120 volt power supply in Canada. Some also use 50 Hertz (cycles per second) frequency versus 60 Hertz in Canada.

♦ Is the product's appearance acceptable in the foreign market, or will you have to make changes? For example, designs incorporating the shape of a cross are not appreciated in many Muslim societies.

♦ If you are planning to export to the United States, will you have to change your product sizes or packaging from metric to Imperial units of measure?

Begin considering the redesign question as early as possible, because if the required changes are too costly you may want to rethink your export plans. Or you may want to limit the countries you will target, depending on the changes they require. If you are unsure of a country's regulations and testing requirements concerning your product, contact your nearest Canadian government International Trade Centre and ask for their assistance. They should be able to provide you with answers, or put you in contact with the appropriate Canadian embassy staff in the target country. (See Appendix B for a listing of Canadian government International Trade Offices.)

3. Cost of New Labelling and Packaging

As in Canada, many countries require specific labelling on the products that are offered to their consumers. For example, food packaging in the United States requires nutrition facts about the product's calorie, fat, sodium, carbohydrate, and protein content. This is in addition to the standard list of ingredients that is sufficient in Canada.

You must also consider the language on the label if you plan to export to a non-English or non-French country. Relabelling can be costly: studies have shown that the French labelling requirement in Canada can add 10 percent to 25 percent to the cost of labelling and packaging. This will give you an idea of the extra costs you might have to face just to comply with language requirements.

You must also be aware of local customs, practices, and religions with regard to labelling. You must be careful about using revealing pictures of men or women on your product, such as on underwear packages, because these may be offensive or even against the law in some countries. Pictures of pigs on your product label will not be well accepted if you are shipping to the Middle East or other Muslim countries.

Packaging requirements differ from country to country. For example, child-proof containers may be required for some products in some countries but not in others. The main issue you will face if you are exporting to the United States concerns complying with the Imperial system of weights and measures instead of the metric system used in almost all of the rest of the world. Along with stating the weights or volumes in ounces, pounds, and quarts, you may also have to manufacture some products in Imperial measurement sizes.

Once again, if you are unsure of the labelling regulations in a particular country, contact your nearest Canadian government International Trade Centre and ask for assistance (see Appendix B).

4. Agent Commissions

The need for some form of local representation in a country will be discussed later in Chapter 10, Retaining an Agent, but no matter what the representation is, it will cost you. A popular form of representation is the commissioned agent. Commissioned agents get paid a percentage of what they sell on your behalf. This percentage varies from country to country, from product to product, and, in some cases, from customer to customer. The commission rates can be as low as 3 percent of the total sales made, or as high as 25 percent or more. The higher rates are usually associated with payoffs or bribes the agent must make in some countries.

You may not be able to estimate the cost of agent commissions until you have some discussions with local representatives. These costs are often simply added directly to your selling price, so that they are flowed through to the customer. Thus, you should not be too concerned about these costs in the early stages of planning.

5. Cost of Getting Paid

The various aspects of export financing vary from letters of credit, which will cost a few percentage points, to having the Canadian Export Development Corporation (EDC) insure your payment at a cost of around 5 percent, depending on the country. In many countries, the EDC can also provide your customers with credit. You will have to add these costs to your price once you find out how much they will be, but at this time estimate about a 5 percent addition to your price. For more information about export financing, see Chapter 5, Financial Issues.

Currency exchange can also be a pitfall. In countries with high inflation rates, the local currency can be severely devalued by the time you exchange it for Canadian dollars. Avoid payment in local currencies if you can. The safest approach is to ask for payment in Canadian dollars, but this is not always possible. A more standard solution is to do the transaction in US dollars, which have become a widely used currency. Then you only have to worry about the minor fluctuations between the US and Canadian dollars. Chances are that some of the components of your product are from the United States, thus reducing the currency risk even more if you quote in US funds.

6. Transportation Costs

You will probably have to quote prices that include delivery costs. These costs will depend on the product and the method of shipment. Perishable goods will have to go by air, as will other products with a short shelf life. It may even be cost effective to ship small electronic products by air. Large or heavy products will probably have to go by sea. However, shipping by sea can incur many additional costs that, when added together, make air shipment attractive.

The best way to answer your transportation questions is to speak to an experienced freight forwarder or shipping agency. They will be able to quote a figure that covers all the associated costs, and will probably offer you several options.

7. Importation Costs

The usual importation costs you will have to face are tariffs and customs charges. Tariffs around the world are gradually being reduced by various trade agreements. For example, the North American Free

Trade Agreement (NAFTA) has reduced tariffs among the United States, Mexico, and Canada to only a few remaining items. For more information about trade through NAFTA, see Chapter 13, North American Free Trade Agreement.

Tariffs in countries outside North America vary considerably. They are usually set up to protect indigenous industry and, in some cases, can be quite high. Your local Canadian International Trade Centre should be able to provide you with information on the tariffs you will face in the countries you are targeting (see Appendix B).

You will probably have to pay brokerage fees to have a customs broker clear your shipment into the country. These fees are usually not too high. However, many countries impose customs charges in addition to tariffs, and they vary with the country and the product. For example, to clear your shipment into Kuwait you will have to pay a 4 percent customs duty plus a 1 percent handling charge. Your shipping agent should be able to inform you of these costs.

8. Installation Costs

If your product requires installation, you will have to consider who will do the installation. It may be quite costly to have your staff do it. You can reduce this cost by using local labour under the supervision of your staff. However, will that local labour be sufficiently skilled, or even available? The issue of installation and setting the product to work will have to be carefully considered and costed.

A popular solution to the installation dilemma is to tie it in with the training of the local operators, the cost of which you include in your quotation. You get paid to train them, and they are then available to do or assist with the installation. Installation and setting the product to work may even be part of the training package.

EXPORTING COSTS LIST

The possible costs you may have to face when you begin exporting are listed here to help you get a better idea of what your total costs will be.

1. Marketing visits
    - airfare
    - lodging
    - meals
    - local transportation
2. Electrical changes
3. Product redesign
4. Label changes
5. Packaging changes
6. Local representative costs and commissions
7. Cost of getting paid
8. Payment insurance
9. Transportation
10. Transportation insurance
11. Tariffs
12. Customs duties
13. Customs charges
14. Customer training
15. Installation

3
LEGAL ISSUES

A number of legal issues may affect some exporters, usually for certain countries. This chapter gives a broad overview of these issues so that you can establish whether or not you should be concerned about them. Checklist 1, the Legal Issues Checklist at the end of the chapter, will help to clarify which legal issues you must contend with. If you have further concerns, additional references are provided at the end of the chapter. Also discussed here are some of the international trade agreements that affect Canada, and the protection of intellectual property.

1. Export Restrictions

Like many countries, Canada controls the import and export of certain products. The authority for this is the Export and Import Permit Act, which dates back to 1953. It is administered by the

Department of Foreign Affairs and International Trade (DFAIT). In effect, it requires export permits for the following three types of products—

♦ those destined for a country on Canada's Area Control List,

♦ those on Canada's Export Control List, and

♦ those of US origin.

These lists are described below.

On their Web site <www.dfait-maeci.gc.ca/~eicb>, DFAIT provides the following list of goods that are under export controls of various degrees:

♦ Agricultural products: refined sugar, sugar-containing products, and peanut butter

♦ Textiles and clothing

♦ Military strategic dual-use goods

♦ Nuclear energy materials and technology

♦ Missile, chemical, or biological goods of non-proliferation concern

♦ Softwood lumber, unprocessed logs, and certain other forest products

♦ Miscellaneous goods, including goods of US origin

♦ All goods destined for countries on the Area Control List

The Area Control List names countries for which an export permit is required for all goods. These are usually countries under sanctions imposed by organizations such as the United Nations. The reasons can vary from human rights violations to support of international terrorism. During the Cold War the list was fairly extensive, but now it is quite short. At the time of writing, the following countries were on the Area Control List:

♦ Angola

♦ Libya

♦ Iraq

The Export Control List deals with goods that require export permits. It is divided into the following eight groups:

Group 1: Dual Use List (items with a civilian/military or nuclear/non-nuclear use)

Group 2:   Munitions List

Group 3:   Nuclear Non-Proliferation List

Group 4:   Nuclear-Related Dual Use List

Group 5:   Miscellaneous Goods

Group 6:   Missile Technology Control Regime List

Group 7:   Chemical and Biological Weapons Non-Proliferation
           List

Group 8:   Chemicals for the Production of Illicit Drugs

The export from Canada of goods of US origin is also controlled under Group 5 of the Export Control List: Miscellaneous Goods. The main reason for this control is to honour US export controls, in particular if the goods are destined for Iran, Iraq, Cuba, or North Korea.

Export permits are obtained by submitting a completed form to DFAIT. The forms are available from DFAIT in Ottawa, or from any International Trade Centre (see Appendix B). DFAIT says they will take only ten working days to process an export permit if it is not military or nuclear related. Permits for military- or nuclear-related products can take several weeks because they have to go through other government departments. Also, permits may be held up for other reasons such as political tensions or conflicts.

2. Import Restrictions

Some countries impose restrictions on the importation of certain goods. For example, it is illegal to bring alcohol or non-Muslim religious articles into Saudi Arabia. It is also illegal to import chewing gum into Singapore, but for reasons more of sanitation than religion. If you suspect a problem with exporting to a particular country, check with the local Canadian embassy staff before you get too far into the export activity.

3. Local Regulations

Many countries regulate the products that are sold to their citizens. This is done for safety reasons, and also to protect local industries from foreign competition. The safety regulations are often enforced by local testing of products, which is done in Canada by the Canadian Standards Association (CSA). In the United States the testing is done by organizations such as the Underwriters Laboratory Inc. (UL). The fact that your product has been approved by the CSA does not necessarily mean that it will pass the regulations and testing in another country. Before you begin marketing to a particular country, find out about their local regulations and product-testing requirements. The Canadian embassy in the country should be able to help you with this.

Regulations to protect indigenous industry can be very subtle, and almost hidden, because this activity is usually counteractive to most international trade agreements. For example, for years Japan had a regulation that required fishing vessels using fish-finding sonar to carry a specially trained sonar operator. The operator was trained to work only a unique Japanese-made sonar display, thus shutting out all other sonar manufacturers around the world.

To agree to export sales, many foreign governments require that some form of reciprocal industry benefit be returned to their indigenous industries. Canada was one of the first countries to use this reciprocal arrangement, and continues to do so, mainly on military purchases. But many other countries have also taken up the practice. For example, the Kuwaiti government requires that, for all contracts more than about five million dollars, the company receiving the contract must invest 30 percent of its value in Kuwait. Ironically, at the time of writing, there is no mechanism in place to administer this law, so it is seldom enforced.

Other countries, such as Korea, will try to get some of the product manufactured in the country. This is a double-edged sword because not only do you lose some business, but you also help set up a competitor. Nevertheless, in order to get the business you may have to agree to such an arrangement. It may not be a problem if you are dealing with rapidly changing technology, because by the time they get set up to manufacture the complete product, you could be on an advanced version that is more popular with customers.

Temporary political issues may affect your business in a country. A good example of this occurred several years ago in Malaysia. The Malaysian government became annoyed with the United Kingdom over something, so they instituted a government purchasing policy referred to as "Buy British Last." Products from the UK could be purchased only if there were no other suppliers. It took a visit from the British Prime Minister to solve the problem.

4. International Trade Agreements

Canada is a member of numerous multilateral trade agreements, bilateral trade agreements, and trade-related memorandums of understanding. Some of these agreements are very important from a trade point of view, while others are merely diplomatic initiatives. The most important agreements for Canadian exporters are the North American Free Trade Agreement (NAFTA) and the World Trade Organization (WTO). NAFTA affects more than 80 percent of Canadian trade, and is thus the most significant agreement. It is discussed in detail in Chapter 13, North American Free Trade Agreement.

The WTO is the only organization that deals with the rules of trade between nations. It replaced the General Agreement on Tariffs and Trade (GATT) in 1995. Whereas the GATT dealt only with the trade of goods, the WTO also includes agreements that cover services and intellectual property. The WTO has about 150 member countries. Its functions include the following:

♦ Maintaining a forum for trade negotiations

♦ Handling trade disputes

♦ Monitoring national trade policies

♦ Offering technical assistance and training for developing countries

5. Intellectual Property Protection

Canada belongs to the Paris Convention for the Protection of Intellectual Property, and a number of similar organizations that protect patents, copyrights, and industrial designs. The following discussion provides definitions of these terms and a brief explanation of the international protection you have on them.

5.1 Patents

Patents protect new technologies (processes, structures, and functions). The Patent Cooperation Treaty (PCT), administered by the World Intellectual Property Organization based in Geneva, assists you in filing patents in other countries. The PCT provides standardized international filing procedures, and under it you can file for a patent in now more than 100 countries. This eases the pressure of the requirement to quickly file an application in another country. Instead, you can file within Canada, in English, and have up to 20 or 30 months to complete the application in other countries.

5.2 Copyrights

Copyrights are for literary, artistic, dramatic, or musical works, as well as software. When you create an original work in Canada you automatically have copyright protection. This also applies to citizens of countries who are signatories to the Berne Convention or the Universal Copyright Convention, or a country that is a member of the World Trade Organization. The copyright is usually held for 50 years after the death of the author, except for photographs, cinematographs, and sound recordings, which are covered for 50 years after they were created.

5.3 Industrial designs

Industrial designs protect the shape, pattern, or ornamentation applied to an industrially produced object. There are no reciprocal agreements between Canada and other countries for the protection of industrial designs.

6. Additional Information

The Internet has a wealth of information on legal issues relating to international business. The following Web sites are well worth exploring and bookmarking for future use. Additional resources are available in print.

1. Export Control Web site of the Canadian government Department of Foreign Affairs and International Trade (DFAIT) at <www.dfait-maeci.gc.ca/~eicb>.

2. Trade Negotiations and Agreements Web site of the Canadian government Department of Foreign Affairs and International Trade (DFAIT) at <www.dfait-maeci.gc.ca/tna-nac>.

3. NAFTA Web site of the Canadian government Department of Foreign Affairs and International Trade (DFAIT) at <www.dfait-maeci.gc.ca/nafta-alena>.

4. Canadian Intellectual Property Office Web site at <cipo.gc.ca>.

5. Patent Cooperation Treaty Web site at <http://www.wipo.org/pct/en/>.

6. World Trade Organization WTO Web site at <http://www.wto.org/.>.

7. Canadian Standards Association Web site at <http://www.csa.ca>.

8. Underwriters Laboratories Inc. Web site at <http://www.ul.com/?>.

9. *Protecting Trade Secrets.* Nishan Swais. Self-Counsel Press, 1996.

CHECKLIST 1
LEGAL ISSUES CHECKLIST

Check off which legal issues apply to you.

Export restrictions

- ❏ Area Control List
- ❏ Export Control List, including goods under US export controls

❏ Import restrictions

Local regulations

- ❏ Approval requirements
- ❏ Testing requirements

❏ Trade agreement implications

Intellectual property protection

- ❏ Patent
- ❏ Copyright
- ❏ Industrial design

4
EXPORT BUSINESS ARRANGEMENTS

There are many business arrangements you can use to enter and continue exporting to a foreign market. This chapter describes the most common business arrangements and, at the end of the chapter, provides Table 1, Business Arrangement Options, which lists your choices. The business arrangement you use will depend on your circumstances and the product you are selling.

1. Selling Direct

Selling direct to end users in foreign countries is not as easy as it seems. You must have the resources to cover the market, as well as an understanding of the different cultures and languages. Some products, such as specialized equipment, systems, or services, however, can be sold directly to the end user in a foreign country if you are able to identify that customer. These sales are usually to a particular type of customer, such as those described below.

1.1 Government buyers

Many countries now have Web sites that identify government departments and contact points. The US government, which is the world's largest purchaser, produces a number of publications to assist vendors in doing business with them. A good place to start is at the US Department of Commerce FedWorld Web site at <www.fedworld.gov>.

1.2 Military buyers

The military of the world require a wide range of goods and services. Except in the United States, these sales are usually conducted with the help of agents. In the United States you can often make direct sales to the purchasing agencies by getting on their lists of potential suppliers and winning subsequent requests for proposals or quotes.

1.3 Large companies

Large companies often buy specialized equipment, systems, and services directly from the vendor without going though agents. The trick is to identify the companies and their buyers. Many large US companies hold special supplier days or trade shows, during which vendors can display their products and meet with company buyers. The trade officials in the Canadian embassy and consulates in the United States will be able to help you identify these opportunities. Large European companies are also major buyers, but usually from other European companies. Large Asian companies, particularly Japanese conglomerates, can be multi-year buyers once you get in with them.

2. Local Marketing Agents

Using a local marketing agent in a foreign country is the most common market-entry approach. Local marketing agents can be in many forms, some of which are described in the following sections. The subject of local marketing agents will be dealt with in much more detail in Chapter 10, Retaining an Agent, where the process of selecting and retaining an agent is explained. The advantages of using agents are that:

- They understand the import business.
- They know the local rules and regulations regarding the importation of goods.
- They know how to deal with the local officials.
- They usually have a full marketing and sales organization to sell foreign goods.

The most common agency arrangement is that of a commissioned agent. This is an individual or company with whom you draw up a contract to represent you in the country or territory. In return for his selling efforts on your behalf, the agent gets a commission or percentage of the values of the sales. Thus, you pay the agent only when he makes a sale for you.

3. Local Distributors

Local distributors are another common export business arrangement, provided that your product lends itself to this approach. Distributors usually purchase your products from you and resell them. Some also stock products and parts, and provide complete installation and repair services. The distributor is usually granted exclusive rights to sell the designated products, in a designated territory, for a designated time period.

Some distributors will purchase the products from you at a wholesale price, and mark up the price as they wish. Others will sell the products at your recommended selling price and, in return, you give them a discount depending on the sales volume. This latter arrangement is advantageous to you if you want to have standard prices throughout the world.

A distributor can make or break your product's reputation in a foreign country. If your distributors stock sufficient spare parts and provide good repair service to customers, they can greatly enhance the reputation of your product. On the other hand, if your distributors cannot support your product adequately, your business will suffer. It is therefore very important to understand the technical capabilities of a potential distributor if you want him to provide installation and repair service for your products. You may have to train your distributor's staff, and maybe even provide him with special tooling. You will want to make sure your distributors will be around for a while, so you should investigate their financial situations as part of your selection process.

4. International Distributors

A growing number of international distributors specialize in selling specific types of products around the world (e.g., security equipment or agricultural equipment). These distributors are usually fairly large companies that represent a number of clients and products in a large number of countries throughout the world. If you can make a suitable arrangement with one of these companies, you will not have to continue working through this book. All you have to do is provide the international distributor with your product, and he will sell it around the world for you.

You may already have run into distributors of this kind as competitors in your home market. Perhaps you should approach these companies to see if they are interested in carrying your product in a foreign market. Negotiations can be difficult because the distributors will want to maximize their own profits. During negotiations, find out if they represent any direct competition to your product, and how they plan to handle this problem. You don't want to sign an exclusive agreement with them only to find out that they put more effort into selling a competing product, in effect locking you out of the marketplace.

5. Local Branch Offices

You may be able to set up a branch office in a foreign country. It would function like most other branch offices, but would probably employ locals who know the local market and local customers. The advantage of this business arrangement is that your company has complete control over pricing, product quality, and other business concerns.

The main disadvantage is that the branch office is subject to the laws of the country, and these vary considerably from country to country. For example, in China it is legal to have a representative office of a foreign parent company. However, it must be sponsored by a Chinese organization that assumes responsibility for the foreign enterprise. Funds to run the activity are channelled from the foreign parent company through the representative office, and income is channelled back to the parent. The Chinese government holds the Chinese sponsor responsible for the representative office.

6. Contractor/Subcontractor Arrangement

In some situations you can simply set up a contractor/subcontractor arrangement with a local company. This is especially true if your product is a component of a larger system, such as an automatic car washer that goes into a specially designed building. A potential buyer who wants to set up the car-wash business will want the complete system, including the building. So you may want to create a relationship in which a local construction company is the prime contractor responsible for the complete installation, including the building, and you simply sell your car-wash equipment to the company as a subcontractor. Prime contractors have complete responsibility for the installation, including meeting the local laws and regulations. They charge what they want for the complete system, and all you have to do is ensure that you get paid for your part of the installation, and that it works.

You will have to be fairly careful in selecting the company you want to work with. Ask yourself the following questions:

- Is the company technically capable of doing the installation?
- Does the company have the finances to see the job through and to pay you?
- Can the company sell the complete system to local customers?

7. Joint Venture Companies

A joint venture company is set up by two or more companies to carry out a business venture in which each of the founding companies has an interest. One of the companies is often from the country to which you plan to export, and thus knows the local laws and regulations, culture and language, and ways of doing business. The founding companies jointly own the joint venture, and share in its profits and losses. The joint venture usually subcontracts back to the founding companies for goods and services associated with the business venture. This type of business arrangement is popular in developing countries because it employs local labour and enhances the country's industrial development.

A major advantage of joint venture companies as a business arrangement is that the joint venture is looked upon as a local company in the country. As such, it will be favoured for future contracts, particularly government contracts. Using China as an example, the government encourages joint ventures with foreign companies and in fact has enacted laws that allow two types of joint ventures: equity joint ventures and cooperative or contractual joint ventures.

7.1 Equity joint ventures

An equity joint venture is a venture in which a new company is formed. It is a legal entity with limited liability equal to the amount of capital contributions the individual partners make. Profits and losses are allocated according to the percentage of capital each partner contributes, and management is shared.

7.2 Cooperative or contractual joint ventures

In a cooperative or contractual joint venture arrangement, no new company is formed. Instead, the partners carry on a joint venture based on contractual arrangements. The contract takes on the status of a separate legal entity. It covers issues such as capital contribution and the distribution of earnings (which is not part of capital contribution). It also covers ownership, management, rights, and liabilities, all which must be negotiated and stated in the contract. The contract usually covers a short period of five to ten years, and at the end of the contract all fixed assets revert to the in-country partner.

Joint ventures have a number of advantages, including the fact that at the dissolution of the contract all assets revert to the local in-country partner. They also have a number of disadvantages, including the typical problem when the local partner becomes overbearing and wants to take complete control. The selection of joint-venture partners must be very carefully made.

8. Strategic Partnering

With the development of large trading blocks such as the North American Free Trade Agreement and other localized trade agreements, it is advantageous to set up strategic partners within these trading blocks. For example, you may set up a strategic business relationship with a company in Germany to give you access to the European market. In return, you provide your German partner with access to the North American market.

Once again, careful selection of a suitable partner is very important. You have to clearly define who does what for whom, and the limitations on the foreign company with regard to marketing in Canada. If you are not careful, there is a danger that your foreign partner may become your competitor in your own country. Nevertheless, strategic partnering is an important business trend that must be considered.

9. Trading Houses

Trading houses are independent companies staffed by international trade experts who act on behalf of client companies. Their main function is to find foreign buyers for their client companies' products. Trading houses can be divided into two general categories: merchants who buy products and then resell them abroad; and agents who sell on commission. Some houses represent offshore clients interested in purchasing certain kinds of goods; some function as cooperatives, representing the products of several producers; and others are export consortia, owned and operated by several producers. Some specialize in a particular foreign market, or deal only with a certain range of products. All trading houses have the following basic operating modes:

- Supply marketing, where they are asked by client manufacturers to find foreign markets for their products
- Demand sourcing, where they are asked by foreign clients to locate suppliers of particular products
- Project procurement by putting together a package of goods and services and bidding it to a project in another country

The services trading houses routinely perform, as specified in the Canadian government Department of Foreign Affairs and International Trade pamphlet entitled "Export Markets: The Trading House Connection," include the following:

- Market identification and selection
- Buyer identification, evaluation (including credit check), and selection
- Identification of product and packaging specifications

- Price negotiations
- Arrangement of terms of sale
- Financial arrangements
- Shipping arrangements
- Preparation of all export documents required
- Protection against export risks
- Payment of goods sold and receipt of payment from foreign buyers
- Satisfaction of claims
- Provision of after-sales service
- Promotional support abroad

More than 500 trading houses operate in Canada, handling more than 50 percent of Canadian exports to countries other than the United States. For more information on trading houses, and to obtain a listing of them, contact organizations such as the Ontario Association of Trading Houses at <www.oath.on.ca> or the Quebec Association of Export Trading Houses at <www.amceq.org/>. You may also want to deal with some of the large international trading houses that service specific areas of the world. An example is Global Sources, based in Hong Kong, which services most of Asia. Global Sources can be contacted through their Web site at <globalsources .com>.

10. Consolidators

Consolidators are companies that act as wholesalers for foreign retailers. For example, many of the consolidators in Miami service the Caribbean and South America. Retailers from these locations buy directly from the consolidators, who assemble large shipments of varied goods and take care of all of the export issues. If your product is very consumer oriented, this is a good way to export it to many countries without much effort. The disadvantages are that the percentages the consolidators charge can be very high, and the competition to get on the consolidator's list can be fierce.

11. Additional Information

The Internet has a wealth of information on export business arrangements. The following Web sites are well worth exploring and bookmarking for future use. Additional resources are available in print.

1. US Department of Commerce FedWorld Web site <www.fedworld.gov>.

2. *Export Markets: The Trading House Connection*, published by the Canadian government and available at the International Trade Centres. Ottawa, 1986.

3. Ontario Association of Trading Houses Web site at <www.oath.on.ca>.

4. Quebec Association of Export Trading Houses Web site at <www.amceq.org/>.

TABLE 1
BUSINESS ARRANGEMENT OPTIONS

1. Selling direct
   - End users
   - Wholesalers
2. Local marketing agent
   - Commissioned agent
   - Retainer agent
3. Local distributor
4. International distributor
5. Local branch office
6. Contractor/subcontractor arrangement
7. Joint venture company
   - Equity
   - Cooperative or contractual
8. Strategic partnering
9. Trading house
10. Consolidator

5
FINANCIAL ISSUES

This chapter examines export pricing structure and strategy. Included in the discussion are financing alternatives, letters of credit, and methods of reducing financial risks. The many services of the Export Development Corporation are also explained.

1. Establishing a Price for Your Product

Your costs in manufacturing a product or providing a service for the domestic market may be quite different from what you encounter in the export world. Calculating your export price is not simply a matter of adding tariff and transportation costs to your domestic charges. As mentioned in Chapter 1, To Export or Not to Export, you may also have to add the costs you will incur in adapting the product to the foreign market. On the positive side, you may qualify for refunds for duty paid on imported goods used in the manufacturing of the product.

As a domestic producer, you would normally calculate your product's price by totalling your costs and adding your profit margin. Costs usually include basic elements such as development, actual production, overhead and operation, promotion (including sales and marketing), and freight forwarding. You will encounter these costs in the export market, plus others. The pricing method you choose will depend on the nature of your product, your size and experience, the characteristics of the market you are targeting, and your long-term goals. Exporters generally employ one of the following three common pricing methods to arrive at their final export price.

1.1 Domestic costs plus

The easiest way to calculate the export price of a product is to subtract your domestic promotion costs and markup from your base domestic price, and then add your export costs plus markup. This is the most common method of arriving at a price, but not the most accurate. It is based on cost figures from previous years, not on current figures, and in no way does it take into account your competition and other conditions in the target market. However, it does allow you to maintain your domestic profit margin.

1.2 Full-cost pricing

For full-cost pricing, take all your domestic costs, minus domestic promotion and markup, add to them all of your exporting costs, and then add your profit margin. This method ensures all of your costs are accounted for. However, it does not take into account your competition or the conditions of the market.

1.3 Marginal cost pricing

Marginal cost pricing, also called the German or Japanese method, is more commonly used by companies that have a well-established domestic operation capable of underwriting fixed costs. You calculate your price based on material, labour, and export-related costs, including modifications, labelling, and promotion. Any amount you charge above this figure is net profit. This method gives you a more accurate idea of the costs and profit attributable to your export activities. It also gives you a lower export price than the domestic cost plus method, and you can adjust this price if you want to. For example, you may want to enter the new market with a lower price, then gradually increase it as you gain market share.

Having a good knowledge and understanding of the target market is a prerequisite to establishing a realistic export price. This means you have to do a thorough market analysis, including an assessment of the potential customers, the actions of your competitors, and your long-term market prospects. Later chapters in this book will help you do this analysis.

2. Pricing Strategy

Once you have established your costs and approximate price, you may need a strategy for your final pricing. When developing your pricing policy, you and your agent or distributor should consider one of the following alternatives.

2.1 Static pricing

You sell your product at the same price to all customers, regardless of who they are, where they live, their socio-economic status, and so on. This approach wins the approval of your customers, but can be undermined by an aggressive competitor who undercuts your price.

2.2 Flexible pricing

You sell your product at various prices, depending on the customer you are targeting. With this approach you increase your revenue, but you risk alienating customers who find out about the variations in your pricing structure.

2.3 Skimming

Skimming is employed only when your product has no competition. You sell at a higher price until the competition enters the market. This approach is also used to determine demand for the product. You start with a higher price and later, based on sales, lower the price accordingly.

2.4 Market penetration

One way to quickly establish your product is to sell at the lowest price possible, without going below cost or "dumping" your product on the market. Hopefully, you will make up for your lower profit margin with increased volume. In the process you eliminate some of the competition; then you can gradually increase your prices.

Your long-range goals play a major part in determining the pricing strategy you should use for a given market. Exporting is not a short-term proposition. You should develop a viable long-term strategy before you enter the market.

3. Methods of Foreign Payment

Your foreign customer can pay you in a number of different ways, some more risky than others. The more popular payment methods are discussed below, beginning with the most risk free and moving toward payment methods that pose more risk to the exporter.

3.1 Advance payment or cash advance

An advance payment or cash advance is the least risky method of payment for the exporter because he or she receives payment before shipping the goods or providing a service. In these days of credit granting, however, advance payments are not common practice. The best you can usually hope for is a percentage down payment on signing the contract or before shipping, with the remaining amount due when the buyer receives the shipment or services. The contract can also call for a series of progress payments during the term of the contract.

3.2 Letter of credit

Letters of credit (L/C) are a very common method of payment, because they reduce the risk for both the seller and the buyer. Some countries insist on the use of letters of credit to pay for foreign goods in order to control foreign exchange. Letters of credit are an important topic and will be dealt with in detail in Section 4.

3.3 Foreign collections

Foreign collections are payments made through a bill of exchange, also called a draft. A bill of exchange looks like a cheque and, like a cheque, it is an order for payment signed by you and made out to your foreign buyer. It specifies the amount the buyer must pay, to whom the payment is to be made, and the date it is due. You instruct your bank to send a draft to the purchaser's bank along with a document conferring ownership of the goods on the buyer. (A draft that is not accompanied by documentation is called a "clean collection.") The draft is then processed in one of two ways:

1. As a sight draft, also called Documents against Payment (D/P), requiring the buyer to pay before receiving the documentation; or

2. As a term draft, also called Documents against Acceptance (D/A), requiring the buyer to accept the draft before receiving documentation and to pay within a set period of time (e.g., 90 days).

In the case of a sight draft or D/P, the buyer's bank holds all documentation until the buyer actually makes payment. This leaves control of the payment and the shipment in your hands. In the case of the term draft or D/A, the buyer is normally required only to confirm the intention to pay in writing before receiving the documentation. This reduces your control of the transaction and leaves you vulnerable to nonpayment. As soon as the buyer pays, his or her bank transfers the funds to your bank, where they are deposited into your account.

In arranging bills of exchange the participating banks serve only as conduits for the two parties engaged in the transaction. Unlike a letter of credit, a bill of exchange is not guaranteed by either bank, nor are the banks responsible for perusing your documents beyond checking to ensure that they conform to the instructions you've provided. In other words, this form of settlement is riskier than the other two methods of payment, but it is sometimes your only alternative in countries in which the banking system is less developed.

3.4 Open accounts

Open accounts operate in much the same way as the running accounts you offer domestic customers. Your buyer places an order and you ship it immediately, along with documentation transferring ownership to the buyer. You then give the buyer a set term to make payment (e.g., within 30 days).

Open accounts obviously favour the buyer and also involve less expense and paperwork for the exporter, but they are risky. You finance the venture yourself, without the backing or guarantee of a bank, and you become a short-term creditor of the buyer. This leaves you with no protection and reduces your cash flow, but it can also make you more competitive.

3.5 Consignment

When you export on consignment, you ship goods abroad but retain ownership until your agent or distributor sells them. In a consignment arrangement, your buyer is heavily favoured since you incur all the expense and risk. Unfortunately it is difficult to manage consignment goods, especially when they are at a distance. Payment is also often delayed, and can be complicated by fluctuating exchange rates. Sales on consignment keep your product moving during a slow market, however, and can be offered to reliable customers in combination with other transactions.

4. Letters of Credit

Letters of credit or documentary credits are a very common method of making payment on international transactions. Letters of credit are an undertaking for payment to the seller, or guarantee of payment, that the buyer's bank makes at the buyer's request. They are a conditional undertaking in which payment is made to you, the exporter, when you have met all of the conditions listed in the letters of credit. These conditions normally include the following:

♦ The provision of goods as specified in the purchase order or agreement

♦ The provision of certain documents, including transport, commercial, and insurance documents, to prove that the order has been shipped

♦ A specific time frame within which the transaction must be completed

♦ Any other conditions the buyer may consider necessary, such as provision of a third-party certificate of inspection completed within a certain period of time, or a health certificate

A letter of credit takes time to complete, but is a very safe method of ensuring payment for your exported product. The steps associated with a letter of credit include the following:

1. The buyer and seller agree on the terms of a transaction, and generate a contract or purchase order.

2. The buyer applies to his or her bank for the letter of credit, providing funds or a loan to cover it, and stating the conditions under which amounts are to be paid to the seller.

3. The buyer's bank forwards the letter of credit to the seller's bank for review and approval by the seller. You, the seller, review it, possibly with the help of your banker and lawyer. If changes need to be made, you negotiate with the buyer to resolve any differences.

4. Once you are happy with the letter of credit, you comply with all of the requirements (such as shipping the goods), and you obtain the necessary documentation to prove the compliance.

5. You present the letter of credit and documentation to your bank.

6. Your bank then sends the documents to the buyer's bank, where they are examined to ensure that they comply with the requirements of the letter of credit. If they do, the buyer's bank transfers the funds to the seller's bank. They also deliver the documents to the buyer.

7. The seller's bank (your bank) transfers the funds into your account.

Letters of credit may be of various types, and you should be wary of some of them:

♦ An irrevocable letter of credit cannot be changed without the seller's consultation and agreement. This is the best form of letter of credit for you, the exporter.

♦ A revocable letter of credit can be cancelled or amended by the issuing bank (the buyer's bank) at any time without informing the seller or beneficiary.

♦ A confirmed letter of credit is one that your bank has confirmed as valid with the issuing bank, and that your bank guarantees payment on, providing that you comply with the conditions.

You can find out more about letters of credit from your bank, or from most Canadian bank Web sites. A good reference is *Documentary Letters of Credit: A Practical Guide*, published by the international trade services of the Bank of Nova Scotia, and available through their Web site at <scotiabank.ca/trade/index.html>.

5. Financing Your Customer

Export financing has been greatly influenced in recent years by the granting of credit to customers. Although this practice was once reserved for only the most established and reliable clientele, it is now an important bargaining chip in contract negotiations between most exporters and foreign buyers. The net result is that exporters now wait longer for payment and are often obliged to make interim financing arrangements with their financial institutions to avoid cash-flow problems. By extending credit you also increase your risk. Reducing that risk should always be your first concern.

Your bank is an important participant in any export negotiation. Canadian chartered banks have traditionally played a key role in financing export sales through their international network of branches, subsidiaries, and correspondent banks. Today that tradition continues, offering a wide range of services tailored to the export community, including —

- loan and collection services;
- information on potential foreign partners and customers;
- advice on market and economic conditions in specific countries; and
- reports on the credit worthiness of particular buyers.

For more information on bank services, consult the many Web sites of Canadian chartered banks, such as those of the Royal Bank of Canada at <royalbank.ca> and the Bank of Nova Scotia at <scotiabank.ca>.

Banks can also loan money to you and your buyer through various methods of promissory notes. They may also buy the buyer's promissory notes and give you immediate cash for them. This process, called factoring, is described in the next section.

Banks can also provide medium- (up to five years) and long-term (up to 15 years) financing for export activities. In this kind of financing, the buyer and his or her business, the foreign market, and the economic and political stability of the country are the main issues governing the transactions. The most common arrangement of this type is when the bank provides buyer credit. Your bank loans money to your buyer for a major project, such as the construction of a factory, and forwards the money to you. The bank and your buyer make an agreement directly with each other, and you have no recourse in the event of delays or problems. To qualify for this kind of financing, the buyer may have to obtain the backing of a government agency or national bank in his or her own country.

6. Factoring

Factoring is the actual purchase of foreign receivables for immediate cash from the exporter, and the collection of money from the buyer. Factors are the companies that carry out this practice. Because factors assume the risk for the account, they conduct a careful check of the buyer's creditworthiness before purchasing the documentation. As the exporter, you do not have to worry about collecting your money because you get it from the factoring company, albeit minus the fee that they charge for the service. Most factoring companies, such as export finance houses, are owned by banks.

Institutions such as export finance houses and factors also provide financing to exporters. Export finance houses buy foreign receivables from exporters and provide a full range of export services, including shipping, documentation, and even financing to the offshore buyer. They charge according to the services requested, and then incorporate the charges into the financial package arranged with the exporter.

7. Reducing the Risk of Foreign Exchange

Currency fluctuations are a major risk area in the international business world. They can sometimes work to your advantage, but they usually work against you. The big problem is the devaluation of currencies in many countries, which is often tied to high inflation rates. If you are paid in the currency of a country that has an annual inflation rate of more than 100 percent, the currency of the country is probably being devalued at the same rate, either by the government of the country or by international currency traders. Thus, even if you arrange the fastest and safest payment method, you could still lose 10 percent or more as you wait for the paperwork to be completed.

The safest situation for you is to arrange the deal in Canadian dollars, but this is not always possible. The next best approach is to quote in, and be paid in, American dollars. This is common practice, since the world is gradually moving toward the US dollar as a standard currency. The Canadian dollar is relatively stable against the US dollar, and chances are that some of the components in your product are imported from the United States, which will reduce the impact of any Canadian currency changes.

Even if your contract is in US dollars, you should still hedge against fluctuations in the relationship between the two currencies. You do this by adding a few percentage points to your price to cover currency-exchange risk. You should also do this if you are dealing in other relatively stable currencies such as British pound sterling or the Eurodollar. Over the years the exchange rates should average out for you. However, if you do have to accept payment in a relatively obscure currency such as the Malaysian ringgit, add a suitably high currency risk factor to your price. Your bank should be able to advise you about what percentage to calculate as a risk factor.

8. Reducing Risk of Non-Payment

You can reduce your risk of non-payment by a foreign buyer in several ways. Most of these should be addressed before you begin your negotiations with a foreign buyer, or possibly even before you begin your marketing efforts.

8.1 Learn about your target market

Spend time researching your foreign market and maintain up-to-date information and data on political and economic conditions, market structure, competitors, government regulations and procedures, tariffs and non-tariff barriers, and domestic transportation, among other concerns. Look into anything that could have a direct or indirect impact on importing your product and the buyer's ability to pay for it.

8.2 Check your customer's credit rating

Always conduct a thorough credit check of your foreign customer before becoming involved in a formal business arrangement. The foreign desk of your bank can help you with credit checks, as can trade staff at your nearest Canadian government International Trade Centre. Commercial services such as Dun & Bradstreet are also available at a small price. Consult their Web site at <www.dnb.ca>.

8.3 Investigate Canadian government programs

The Export Development Corporation (EDC) can insure your exports against non-payment for a variety of reasons, including buyer insolvency and political problems. Section 9. explains the services the EDC offers.

8.4 Explore your financial options

The payment alternatives commonly used by foreign buyers and their Canadian suppliers to settle short-term accounts are based on the type of product being purchased, the size of the order, and a number of other factors. In general, the more risk-free an alternative is for the buyer, the more risk it entails for the supplier, and vice versa. Your negotiations will thus require compromise by both sides, but you should be prepared. By exploring each alternative carefully, perhaps in consultation with your banker, you can develop a financial strategy that will minimize your risk.

8.5 Specify financial and payment details in the contract

Remember that a sales contract is a legal document enforceable by law. However, it is only as good as the laws of the country you are dealing with. Nevertheless, you should detail the financial arrangements in the contract, in particular the payment terms, so that it is quite clear to your buyer what you expect from him or her.

8.6 Establish a balanced credit policy with your buyer

In today's competitive marketplace, your credit package can mean the difference between negotiating a successful contract and losing out to a more flexible competitor. Formulate a policy with which you are comfortable, bearing in mind factors such as the value of the contract, the policies of your competitors, the stability of the market, common practices in the market, and the availability of insurance coverage. Once you have a policy in place, you can establish a credit ceiling, payment terms, and a suitable collection approach.

9. Canadian Export Development Corporation

The Export Development Corporation (EDC) is a Canadian crown corporation that has been assisting Canadian exporters since 1944. Information on the services the EDC offers can be obtained through their Web site at <www.edc.ca>. The following is a summary of the main services of the EDC.

9.1 Insurance

The EDC's insurance covers up to 90 percent of losses due to non-payment by a foreign buyer as a result of commercial or political risk. Included under these two risk categories are buyer default or insolvency, blockage of funds transfer, war and rebellion, cancellation of the buyer's importing licence, or cancellation of your own export permit from the Canadian government. There is no restriction on the size of the company that can apply, and almost any export transaction can be covered as long as the Canadian content is 50 percent or greater.

Within the EDC's short- and medium-term policy categories are some 20 types of insurance- and performance-related guarantees. New exporters will be particularly interested in the global comprehensive insurance, which is a one-year renewable policy that covers all export sales, except those specifically excluded by the EDC. (The exclusions vary from contract to contract and are usually listed in the insurance contract.) Also available are bank documentary credit insurance and bulk agricultural insurance for large shipments of seasonal agricultural products.

9.2 Export financing

The EDC can provide financing for up to 85 percent of the total value of a shipment's Canadian content. These funds are forwarded directly to the exporter on behalf of the buyer or borrower, making the transaction equivalent to a cash sale to the exporter. The loan arrangements vary from case to case, but generally involve the following:

(a) Direct loan

    The loan is usually for a single export transaction, once the financing arrangements have been agreed to by the contracting parties. Funds are dispersed under a disbursement agreement signed by the exporter, the buyer, and the EDC.

(b) Note purchase

The EDC purchases the foreign buyer's promissory note from the Canadian exporter.

(c) Specialized credit

Specialized credit is a financial arrangement for Canadian goods a Canadian company purchases for permanent use outside Canada, or for lease to another company that intends to use the goods on a permanent basis outside Canada.

9.3 Lines of credit

Lines of credit are loans extended to reliable foreign borrowers, such as banks or government corporations, for the financing of a series of unspecified transactions within a broad business category. The funds are allocated as a particular project proceeds and transactions are identified. Information on EDC lines of credit is available from the EDC itself, the International Trade Centres, the commercial section of the Canadian embassies, and from various government publications. If your product is within the business category of the line of credit, you may be able to take advantage of it.

10. Additional Information

The Internet has a wealth of information on international finance issues. The following Web sites are well worth exploring and bookmarking for future use. Additional resources are available in print.

1. "Roadmap to Exporting: Guide to Federal Government Services." Export Development Corporation, 1999. Available on the EDC Web site at <www.infoexport.gc.ca/businesswomen/menu-e.asp>.

2. *Documentary Letters of Credit: A Practical Guide,* published by the International trade services of the Bank of Nova Scotia, and available on their Web site at <scotiabank.ca/trade/index.html>.

3. Royal Bank of Canada Web site at <royalbank.ca>.

4. Bank of Nova Scotia Web site at <scotiabank.ca>.

5. Dun & Bradstreet Web site <www.dnb.ca>.

6. Export Development Corporation Web site <www.edc.ca>.

6
GOVERNMENT AND
OTHER ASSISTANCE

This chapter outlines some of the federal, provincial, and other sources of assistance available to the Canadian exporter.

1. Federal Government Assistance

The Canadian government has International Trade Centres in every province across Canada to assist Canadian exporters. (See Appendix B for the listing of these offices.) These centres have trade-related libraries with many free-of-charge publications on different aspects of the exporting process. They also have staff to counsel companies interested in becoming exporters. They can provide information on target markets, and can provide you with information on government programs that assist exporters. One such program is the Program for Export Market Development (PEMD). Because of its importance to the novice exporter, the Program for Export Market Development is described in detail in Section 3.

The International Trade Centres can also put you in touch with the right people in the Trade Commissioner Service within the Canadian embassies abroad. These trade commissioners act as the Canadian government's front-line troops in the international marketplace. The services they offer include the following.

1.1 Market prospects

The Trade Commissioner Service will help you assess your potential target market and provide:

- Advice on doing business in the market;
- An indication of major barriers, regulations, and certifications;
- Notification of upcoming events (trade fairs, conferences, seminars, trade missions); and
- Suggested next steps.

1.2 Key contacts search

The trade commissioners in the embassies have local knowledge of key contacts. They can provide information about:

- Potential buyers, potential partners, or both;
- Agents;
- Distributors and importers;
- Consultants;
- Government officials;
- Associations and chambers of commerce;
- Freight forwarders;
- Lawyers;
- Technology sources; and
- Financial institutions.

1.3 Local company information

The Trade Commissioner Service can provide information about local companies that you have identified and want to know more about.

1.4 Visit information

Once you decide to visit a country, the Trade Commissioner Service can provide practical advice on timing and organizing your trip, including information about:

- Local hotels;
- Business support services;
- Interpreters and translators; and
- Local transportation.

1.5 Face-to-face briefings

You can arrange to meet with the appropriate Canadian official in the embassy to discuss the most recent developments in the target market, your potential market, the approach you should consider, and so on.

2. Internet Contacts for Other Government Departments

Various Canadian government departments make considerable information about international business available on the Internet. The most significant one is the Department of Foreign Affairs and International Trade (DFAIT) Infoexport site at <www.infoexport.gc.ca>, which provided a source for some of the information in this chapter. Another good Web site is the Industry Canada Strategis site at <http://strategis.ic.gc.ca>. Other useful government departments, agencies, and crown corporations include:

1. Team Canada Inc.

   Team Canada Inc. (TCI) is a virtual trade network of government departments and agencies dedicated to helping Canadian business succeed in world markets. It can be reached by phoning toll-free 1-888-811-1119, or by visiting their Web site at <www.exportsource.gc.ca>.

2. Atlantic Canada Opportunities Agency

   The Atlantic Canada Opportunities Agency (ACOA) serves Nova Scotia, New Brunswick, Prince Edward Island, and Newfoundland and Labrador. You can visit their Web site at <www.acoa.ca>.

3. Canada Economic Development for Quebec Regions Program

   The Canada Economic Development for Quebec Regions Program (CED) serves Quebec. You can visit their Web site at <www.dec-ced.gc.ca>.

4. Federal Economic Development Initiative for Northern Ontario

   The Federal Economic Development Initiative for Northern Ontario (FedNor) offers programs and services that bring economic benefit to communities in northern Ontario. You can find out more about them on their Web site at <www.fednor.ic.gc.ca>.

5. Western Economic Diversification Canada

   Western Diversification (WD) promotes the development and diversification of the economy of Western Canada, including Manitoba, Saskatchewan, Alberta, and British Columbia. Their programs and services are described on their Web site at <www.wd.gc.ca>.

6. Agriculture and Agri-Food Canada

   The Agri-Food Trade Service (ATS) is an international business development service for Canadian agri-food exporters. ATS provides a single point of access to a range of government services, including international market information and export counselling tailored to the agriculture and agri-food industries. Their Web site is at <http://ats.agr.ca>. The ATS can also be contacted by toll-free telephone at 1-888-811-1119.

7. Aboriginal Business Canada

   Aboriginal Business Canada (IC) helps aboriginal-owned companies grow their businesses and build export sales. They have offices located across Canada. Their Web site is <www.abc.gc.ca>.

8. Export Development Corporation

   The Export Development Corporation (EDC) is more fully explained in Chapter 5 (Financial Issues). Their Web site is at <www.edc.ca>.

9. Business Development Bank

The Business Development Bank (BDC) offers a variety of products and services to help small businesses grow. They can be contacted by toll-free telephone at 1-888-463-6232. Their Web site is at <www.bdc.ca>.

10. Forum for International Trade Training

The Forum for International Trade Training (FITT) provides training in international business. They can be contacted by toll-free telephone at 1-800-561-3488. Their Web site is at <www.fitt.ca>.

3. Program for Export Market Development

The Program for Export Market Development (PEMD) is the Canadian government's cornerstone international business development program. Since its inception in 1971, PEMD has assisted more than 28,000 Canadian businesses in marketing their goods and services abroad. Sales stemming from PEMD-supported activities have exceeded $12 billion.

Details of the PEMD can be obtained at any International Trade Centre (see Appendix B), or through their Web site at <www.infoexport.gc.ca/section2/export_menu-e.asp>, the source of much of the information in this section. PEMD reduces the company risk of entering a foreign market by sharing the cost of international marketing activities, on a repayable basis. It is not a grant, but rather a repayable contribution based on sales the recipient company makes in the country or project designated in the PEMD contract. If no sales are made, the contribution is not repaid. The PEMD has four major elements, each of which is briefly described below.

3.1 Market development strategies

PEMD's Market Development Strategies (MDS) provide financial assistance for a package of support visits, trade fairs, and marketing support initiatives, based on the company's one-year to two-year international marketing plan. Companies are limited to one approved application in a twelve-month period, and one application per target market. In the case of exporting to the United States, up to three applications, each for a separate and distinct region, may be approved.

The PEMD annual contribution per application is a minimum of $5,000 and a maximum of $50,000. Costs that can be shared on a 50 percent basis include the following:

- ◆ Costs of return economy international airfare, or equivalent transportation costs to visit the target market;
- ◆ Costs of participating at trade fairs in the target market;
- ◆ Costs of return economy international airfare or equivalent transportation for foreign buyers to visit the company's Canadian facilities;
- ◆ Costs of product testing by foreign standards agencies for market certification;
- ◆ Legal fees for marketing agreements abroad;
- ◆ Costs of labelling to meet label compliance requirements;
- ◆ Costs of return economy international airfare, or equivalent transportation costs for offshore company trainees to travel to Canada;
- ◆ Costs of product demonstration or solo show; and
- ◆ Costs of the production of video, literature, brochure, or promotional material that is specifically designed for a target market.

3.2 New-to-exporting companies

PEMD also supports companies that have an insufficient knowledge of exporting, or lack in-house financial or human resources. It provides financial assistance for one market visit or trade fair participation so that companies can decide whether they should develop an export capability, or whether their product is exportable to a particular market. Companies are limited to one approved application in a 12-month period, to an overall maximum of three approvals, each to a different market. The PEMD contribution per application is a maximum of $7,500. Costs that can be shared on a 50 percent basis include the following:

- ◆ Costs of return economy international airfare or equivalent transportation costs for an approved market identification visit; and
- ◆ Costs of participating in an international trade fair outside Canada.

3.3 Capital projects bidding

Another PEMD element supports bidding on capital projects or proposal preparation at the pre-contractual stage. It is designed to assist Canadian firms in bidding for major capital projects outside Canada, against foreign competition. The bid or proposal must be for the supply of Canadian goods, and for services such as engineering, construction, architecture, and management consulting. It must be for a defined project greater than one million dollars. Companies are limited to two approved applications in a 12-month period; however, the maximum contribution in a year may not exceed $50,000. The maximum PEMD contribution per capital project is $50,000. Eligible costs include the following:

♦ In lieu of expenses, a per diem allowance of $150 while travelling outside Canada ($250 in Japan and $200 in Taiwan, South Korea, Hong Kong, and Singapore), for the applicant's professional employees working on the bid preparation and other aspects of the project.

Costs that can be shared on a 50 percent basis include the following:

♦ Costs of return economy international airfare or equivalent transportation costs for company officials or incoming potential clients to Canada or to another approved location.

♦ The following costs are allowed under the program, if they are incurred at arms' length to the applicant:

• Costs of printing, computer, and word processing;

• Costs of legal and translation services;

• Costs of international courier, freight, and shipping for project documents and supporting material;

• Costs of obtaining bid or performance bonds;

• Costs of purchasing bid or tender documents; and

• Consultants' fees and expenses (up to a maximum of 25 percent of the total PEMD contribution).

3.4 Trade association activities

Another PEMD element is intended for national, major-trade, or industry associations of a non-sales and sector-specific or horizontal nature. Activities undertaken by the association must be part of a long-term international business plan and must be for the benefit of the association members and the industry. The long-term strategy or plan may include activities relating to the generic promotion of the industry association's products or services, improved market access, or generation of market intelligence and information for the benefit of the industry.

4. Provincial Government Assistance

All of the provincial governments have some form of program to help exporters in their provinces. Some are more useful than others. Here is a listing of provincial contact points and, where applicable, a brief description of export programs you may want to look into.

4.1 Alberta

Information on international business opportunities, market profiles, trade events calendars, and other export-related topics can be found at the Alberta government Investment and Trade Division of Department of Economic Development Web site at <www .alberta-canada.com/dept/invtrd.cfm>. You can contact them by toll-free telephone anywhere in Alberta at 310-0000.

4.2 British Columbia

The BC government makes available information on trade and export through its BC Trade and Investment Office. Find our more about them through their Web site at <www.cse.gov.bc.ca /DoingBusiness/BCGovernmentLinks/bctio.htm>. You can contact them by toll-free telephone anywhere in British Columbia through Enquiry BC at 1-800-663-7867.

4.3 Manitoba

The Manitoba Trade and Investment Corporation has some interesting programs, including one that will provide financial assistance in developing brochures for exporting your product, and one to assist you in developing an Internet site. Visit their Web site at <www.gov.mb.ca/itt/trade/index.html>. You can reach them toll free by telephone within North America at 1-800-529-9981.

4.4 New Brunswick

Incentive grants for 50 percent of project costs up to a maximum of $5,000 per project are available to assist New Brunswick companies in exporting. Information on this and other programs can be obtained from the Department of Investment and Exports Web site at <www.gnb.ca/Inv-Exp/ia-ie.aspm>. You can also get information from New Brunswick Business by toll-free telephone anywhere in New Brunswick at 1-800-668-1010.

4.5 Newfoundland and Labrador

The Newfoundland and Labrador government leads trade missions, particularly to New England, encouraging local companies to explore business prospects in the Eastern United States. Information on this and other programs can be obtained from the Newfoundland and Labrador Department of Industry, Trade, and Rural Development Web site at <www.success.nfld.net/>.

4.6 Northwest Territories

With several new diamond mines expected to open in the next 10 years, the government of the Northwest Territories recognizes the potential of this region to become North America's primary diamond exporter. The government's Diamond Project provides financial incentives to add value and create employment in diamond polishing and manufacture. As well, the government provides support to northern manufacturers in other sectors to encourage export development or import replacement to increase self-sufficiency. You can find out more about assistance available on the Northwest Territories Department of Resources, Wildlife, and Economic Development Web site at <www.gov.nt.ca/RWED/>.

4.7 Nunavut

The Nunavut government department for sustainable development works with partners to develop a strong sustainable resource exploration and development sector. You can find out more about their financial incentives for exporting at <www.gov.nu.ca/sd.htm>

4.8 Nova Scotia

The Nova Scotia Export Development Corporation creates export opportunities for Nova Scotia businesses (see their Web site at <www.novascotiabusiness.com/expttr/ETtop.htm>). As well, Nova Scotia Business Inc., a crown corporation, focuses on export promotion, investment attraction, business retention and expansion, and business financing. You can find out more about this program on their Web site at <www.novascotiabusiness.com> or by toll-free telephone within Nova Scotia at 1-877-297-2124.

4.9 Ontario

Ontario Exports Inc. is the Trade Development Division of the Ministry of Economic Development and Trade. It works with Ontario companies to develop new exporting opportunities, and assists foreign buyers in finding Ontario suppliers for their purchasing requirements. They also provide a number of export education and trade promotion programs. More information can be found at their Web site at <www.ontario-canada.com/export>, or you can contact them toll-free by telephone anywhere in Ontario at 1-877-468-7233.

4.10 Prince Edward Island

Exporting activities are accelerating in Prince Edward Island, with local companies finding and developing new markets. Prince Edward Island Business Development along with the Atlantic Canadian Opportunities Agency organizes trade missions to support Island companies in expanding their markets. You can find out more on their Web site at <http://www.peibusinessdevelopment.com/trade/index .php3>.

4.11 Quebec

The Quebec ministère de l'Industrie et du Commerce maintains a complete information and service centre on its Web site is at <www.mic.gouv.qc.ca/commerce-exterieur/index.html>.

4.12 Saskatchewan

The Saskatchewan Economic and Co-operative Development Department has a number of export related programs. Information on these can be obtained at their Web site at <www.gov.sk.ca/govt /econdev/>.

4.13 Yukon

The Yukon government facilitates export trade as a means of supporting increased and more diversified economic activity in the territory. You can find out more about Yukon's export policy on the Yukon Economic Development Web site at <www.economicdevelopment.yk.ca/>.

5. Trading Houses

Trading houses can provide a variety of services to the exporter. Their activities are more fully explained in Chapter 4, Export Business Arrangements.

6. Banks

Most of Canada's banks have an international trading section with extensive services for importers and exporters. Many also publish general information guides on export financing, and provide information on their Web sites. Two such sites are the Royal Bank of Canada's Web site at <http://royalbank.ca> and the Bank of Nova Scotia's Web site at <http://scotiabank.ca>.

7. Chambers of Commerce and Boards of Trade

In most countries, chambers of commerce and boards of trade serve to develop and stimulate private business. They do so in a variety of ways, including through seminars, workshops, and personal advice on how to get involved in exporting. You can usually obtain information about who to contact within these organizations in a particular country through the country's embassy in Canada. They will be quite happy to discuss business with you, especially if it involves business for their member companies.

8. International Business Groups

With Canada's growing ethnic diversity, business organizations have emerged to represent the interests of dozens of ethnic groups and to strengthen economic ties with their countries of origin. Members of these groups have valuable linguistic skills and cross-cultural business expertise, and can act as consultants to Canadian exporters.

They may also have contacts with similar ethnic groups in countries other than their home nation, thus expanding their capability and influence.

9. Additional Information

The Internet has a wealth of information about government and other assistance. The following Web sites are well worth exploring and bookmarking for future use. Additional resources are available in print.

1. Canadian government Industry Canada Strategis site at <http://strategis.ic.gc.ca>.

2. Canadian government Department of Foreign Affairs and International Trade (DFAIT) Infoexport site at <www.infoexport.gc.ca>.

3. Canada Export Development Corporation, "Roadmap to Exporting: Guide to Federal Government Services." Ottawa, 1999. Available on their Web site at <www.infoexport.gc.ca/businesswomen/menu-e.asp>.

4. Royal Bank of Canada Web site at <http://royalbank.ca>.

5. Bank of Nova Scotia Web site at <http://scotiabank.ca>.

6. Export Development Corporation Web site at <www.edc.ca>.

7. Team Canada Inc Web site at <www.exportsource.gc.ca>.

8. Atlantic Canada Opportunities Agency Web site at <www.acoa.ca>.

9. Canada Economic Development for Quebec Regions Program Web site at <www.dec-ced.gc.ca>.

10. Federal Economic Development Initiative for Northern Ontario Web site at <www.fednor.ic.gc.ca>.

11. Western Diversification Web site at <www.wd.gc.ca>.

12. Agriculture and Agri-Food Canada Web site at <http://ats.agr.ca>. They can be contacted in Ottawa by telephone at 613-759-7687, or by fax at 613-759-74499.

13. Aboriginal Business Canada Web site at <www.abc.gc.ca>.

14. Business Development Bank Web site at <www.bdc.ca>. They can be contacted by toll-free telephone at 1-888-463-6232.

15. Forum for International Trade Training (FITT) Web site <www.fitt.ca>. They can be contacted by toll-free telephone at 1-800-561-3488.

16. PEMD information Web site <www.infoexport.gc.ca/section2/export_menu-e.asp>.

17. Alberta Investment and Trade Division of Department of Economic Development Web site at <www.alberta-canada.com/dept/invtrd.cfm>.

18. British Columbia Trade and Investment Office Web site at <www.cse.gov.bc.ca/DoingBusiness/BCGovernmentLinks /bctio.htm>.

19. Manitoba Trade and Investment Corporation Web site at <www.gov.mb.ca/itt/trade/index.html>.

20. New Brunswick government Web site at <www.gov.nb.ca/edt/econdev.asp>.

21. Newfoundland and Labrador Department of Industry, Trade and Rural Development Web site at <www.success.nfld.net>.

22. Northwest Territories Department of Resources, Wildlife, and Economic Development Web site at <www.gov.nt.ca/RWED/>.

23. Nova Scotia Export Development Corporation Web site at <www.novascotiabusiness.com/expttr/ETtop.htm>

24. Nova Scotia Business Inc. Web site at <www.novascotiabusiness.com>.
    Nova Scotia government Web site at <www.gov.ns.ca/>.

25. Ontario Exports Inc., the Trade Development Division of the Ministry of Economic Development and Trade, Web site at <www.ontario-canada.com/export].

26. Prince Edward Island Business Development Web site at <http://www.peibusinessdevelopment.com/trade /index.php3>.

27. The Quebec ministère de l'Industrie et du Commerce Web site at <www.mic.gouv.qc.ca/commerce-exterieur/index.htm>.

28. Saskatchewan Economic and Co-operative Development government department Web site at <www.gov.sk.ca/govt/econdev/>.

29. Yukon Economic Development Web site at <www.economicdevelopment.yk.ca/>.

7
MARKET STUDY

To help you decide on an international market for your product, you should carry out a market study. You should do this even if you are fairly certain of the particular export market you want to target. The study will help you focus your thinking and force you to ask some hard questions about the market. The answers to these questions may cause you to change your mind. You may decide to abandon a particular market area, to go after it sooner, or, in all likelihood, to alter your approach to it. This chapter discusses the various aspects of an international market study.

1. What Is a Market Study?

A market study should analyze the international market for your particular product to determine the best market area to which you should direct your resources. If properly done, it will eliminate markets with very little profit potential and highlight those that are worth going after. A market study often includes a marketing plan, discussed in detail in Chapter 8, Market-Entry Planning.

Many books discuss market studies and analysis. This book touches on aspects peculiar to the international market, including the following:

♦ International user benefits

♦ International buyer segmentation

♦ Competition, both direct and indirect

♦ Country segmentation

♦ International market potential

2. International User Benefits

Customers buy a product if it is of some benefit to them. The benefit can range from intangible to highly practical. For example, a few years ago wealthy Russian consumers were clamouring to buy American Levi jeans. To these people, there was an intangible benefit in owning them, and they would even offer to buy the jeans from US tourists on the street. At the more tangible end of the scale of user benefits, the export of a good heating system to a northern country such as Norway meets a highly practical user benefit and may be a more practical business endeavour, as well.

When considering user benefits, it is important to distinguish between the benefits derived from the product and the features of the product. Features are what the product is designed to do. For example, a software accounting program may have a feature that enables you to write cheques. But if you prefer not to write cheques electronically, this feature is of no benefit to you. Benefits are aspects of a product that appeal to the buyer.

In order to identify a suitable international market for your product, you must consider how the product would be beneficial to potential customers in the market you are considering. The following are some questions you might want to ask yourself:

♦ Does your product have unique features that would be beneficial to a particular group of customers, from their point of view?

- Does your product provide more benefits to the user than the competition's product? (Answer this question from the international customer's perspective, not from that of your designers, who will be biased by the features they have put into the product.)
- Does your product solve the customer's problem?
- Is your product cost effective?
- What other intangible aspects of your product might appeal to the international customer?

The answers to these and similar questions will tell you if the market you are considering is right for you. The answers will also indicate how you should structure your approach to marketing and advertising.

3. International Buyer Segmentation

Once you have identified the benefits that international users would derive from your product, you then have to identify the customer segments or groups that contain these users. There are several ways to do this segmentation, depending on your product. Generally, you should look at each country or region you are considering from the following perspectives.

3.1 Benefits derived

Segment the market according to the user benefits you established earlier. What parts of the world contain the most customers who would benefit from your product? Depending on the product, this analysis should considerably narrow the field.

3.2 Economic concerns

Your next concern is to segment the potential buyers into groups or countries that can afford your product. It is probably not a wise move to try to sell luxury items to the consumers of impoverished Bangladesh. If your product is very consumer oriented, you should choose countries or other international segments with high per-capita income. You may also want to consider a number of other factors that are listed later in this chapter in Worksheet 2, the Country Evaluation Worksheet.

3.3 Geographical concerns

The size of a country or region could make a difference in your selection of a target market. The sales potential of some products differs enormously between small and large populations. For example, products that sell to households will have more sales potential in a country with a larger population. However, sales of a specialized product such as an air traffic control system will not depend on the size of the population but on the number of airports in the country.

The physical details of a region will also affect the sale of some products. For example, umbrellas will not be a big seller in regions that have a dry desert climate. If the geography of a country affects your product, a good atlas will enable you to identify segments of the world that could contain your future customers.

3.4 Political concerns

The stability of the government and its attitude toward business should also be considered. You don't want to waste your effort on a region that could erupt in civil war.

3.5 Sociological concerns

Social conditions such as religion and ethnic background can play an important role in your market segment decision. For example, if your product helps to increase the production of hogs, you can eliminate marketing to Israel and the Moslem countries where pork is against their religion. Another sociological issue can be the gap between rich and poor. Mexico has an inordinately high number of millionaires and even billionaires, yet a major part of the population lives in poverty. So you may successfully sell luxury goods to Mexico despite its general poverty.

3.6 Demographics

Demographic aspects of consumers such as age, occupation, gender, and home ownership are important for some products. This data may not be available in sufficient detail for your potential target countries. However, you can get considerable information from the US Central Intelligence Agency's *World Fact Book*, which has information about all the countries of the world. You can access this data through their Web site at <www.odci.gov/cia/publications/factbook>.

3.7 Lifestyle

Customer lifestyle is an important consideration for some products, such as electronics, clothing, and leisure products. If you manufacture high-end ski clothing, you will probably find many more customers in Sweden, where recreational skiing is a way of life, than in the snow-covered mountains of Tibet.

3.8 Purchasing habits

Will consumers be loyal to a particular brand or to a particular country of origin? For example, for years Coca-Cola was not available for sale in many Arab countries, apparently because the head of the company was Jewish. You can research the potential for similar problems by contacting the Canadian trade official in the country of interest.

By now you will have narrowed your potential world market to a manageable number of countries or regions that you want to explore in more detail. The next step is to look at the competition in these remaining countries or regions.

4. Competition

Your competition in a country or region can be either direct or indirect. Indirect competition is another way of solving the customer's problem. For example, very inexpensive labour is indirect competition to labour-saving devices. Some other types of indirect competition to consider include the following:

- ♦ Technology substitution, such as fibre optic cables replacing copper wires for data transmission;
- ♦ Processes that can be substituted for expensive equipment;
- ♦ Import restrictions the government applies to protect local industry;
- ♦ Government regulations that effectively bar your product; and
- ♦ Apathy, or the feeling of not wanting to make a change.

Direct competition comes from the companies that manufacture or distribute a product similar to yours. In the international market this might be quite different from the competition you must deal with at home. You can identify the competition, and get information on them, in several ways, including:

- Internet searches;
- Trade shows;
- Trade publications;
- Conferences;
- Agents;
- Customers; and
- Your suppliers.

Once you have identified the competition in an export market you are thinking of targeting, assess their strengths and weaknesses in comparison with your company and your product. If the competition is too strong, you may have to decide against that particular market area. If the competition is weak or if it seems manageable, you may decide to direct the information you have gathered toward your marketing approach, advertising, and pricing. Some of the aspects you should consider about competition in your export market include:

- Product features and performance;
- User benefits;
- Applications;
- Packaging;
- Servicing;
- Price;
- Market share;
- Technical support; and
- Competing company's financial situation.

When you are assessing the competition, remember to consider how they may react to your market presence. For example, they could drop their prices, which could have an immediate effect on your market-entry plans. If you have a superior product, how long will it take your competitor to bring out an equivalent product? Can they apply other pressures to squeeze you out of the market, such as a disinformation campaign? All of these issues and many more are real threats in the international marketplace. If you discover the potential for these threats in a country or region, you may want to avoid that market.

5. Country Segmentation

You should now have narrowed your search to a few possible countries to which to target your product. You will not be able to effectively target all of them at the same time, so you will have to prioritize them. The best way to do this is to set up a matrix that lists evaluation criteria and provides columns in which to record your assessment of each country. Worksheet 1, at the end of this chapter, is a Country Evaluation Worksheet that you can use. For each country, work down the list of evaluation criteria and assess the effect of that criteria on your potential sales in the country. Because this is a very subjective process, you will not be able to quantify it exactly. The best you can do for each criterion is to evaluate the effect it will have on your sales — bad, moderate, good, or very good. When you are finished, add up all of the evaluations and average them into one composite bad, moderate, good, or very good evaluation for that particular country.

Make sure that your evaluation is based on how the criteria will affect your sales. For example, the benefits derived from a heating system will probably be "very good" in Norway, "good" in northern China, "moderate" in Korea, and "bad" in Singapore. On the other hand, the competition will be high in Norway, so the overall evaluation of the effect that the Norwegian competition has on your product might be "bad."

Most of the evaluation criteria listed in Worksheet 1 have already been discussed, but there are some additional points that you should address as you prioritize each criterion. They are briefly described below.

5.1 Regulatory issues

As discussed in Chapter 4, Export Business Arrangements, some countries may have product regulations and testing requirements that make it difficult for you to enter their markets. Assess these issues based on how much trouble you will have to go through to get into the market. If you have to do extensive testing, then the evaluation would be "bad." If you must only complete some additional paperwork on your already acquired Canadian Standards Association or Underwriters' Laboratories Inc. approval, then assess it as "moderate." And if there are no regulations, then you can assess the criteria as "very good."

5.2 Ease of access

How easy is it to get into the market, based on issues like travel time, travel cost, and frequency of visits required?

5.3 Product redesign

Do you have to make changes to your product to enter the market, such as changes to the electrical requirements or a complete redesign, relabelling, or repackaging?

6. Market Potential

You should try to gauge the potential market for your product in a particular country or region in order to indicate the probable sales you can achieve. For the purposes of this assessment, since it is relative from country to country, consider market potential as the number of potential product sales if there were no competition, and if everyone who wanted to buy your product did so. Although this number will probably be large for each of the countries to which you are interested in exporting, unfortunately there is no way you will get all of that business.

You now have to assess the probable or real market that you can expect for your product. This is where the information you have gathered about each country becomes vital. Use this information to get a realistic assessment of the market you can hope to win. There are many ways of doing this assessment, but all are subjective. The simplest approach is to take the total potential market figure you calculated, and estimate the percentage of actual sales that will take place, based on the information you have about the country. Then consider the competition. Make an estimate of what percentage of the business each competitor will get, and how much you can expect. Multiply this percentage by the market potential and you will have a relative idea of what your probable sales will be in that particular market.

Remember, you are only after a relative rating of each country. The calculations do not have to be perfectly accurate, but should use the same method for each country. With this relative figure for the probable market in each country, you can rank the countries in order of priority, with the highest market first, of course. This simple approach will give you a relative idea about which country or countries to target initially in your international export efforts.

7. Additional Information

The Internet has a wealth of information on market studies. The following Web sites are well worth exploring and bookmarking for future use. Additional resources are available in print.

1. *Marketing Your Product.* Donald Cyr and Douglas Gray. Self-Counsel Press, 1998.

2. *Marketing Your Service.* Jean Withers and Carol Vipperman. Self-Counsel Press, 1998.

3. US Central Intelligence Agency *World Fact Book.* Available through their Web site at <www.odci.gov/cia/publications/factbook>.

4. Canadian Industry Canada Strategis Market Research Web site at <strategis.ic.gc.ca/sc_mrkti/ibinddc/engdoc/1a1.htm>.

5. *Look Before You Leap: Market Research Made Easy.* Don Doman, Dell Dennison, and Margaret Doman. Self-Counsel Press, 1993.

WORKSHEET 1
COUNTRY EVALUATION WORKSHEET

Evaluation Criteria	Country A	Country B	Country C
1. Benefits derived from product			
2. Economic situation			
a. Gross Domestic Product (GDP)			
b. Per capita income			
c. Current rate of growth			
d. Projected rate of growth			
3. Geography			
a. Size			
b. Climate			
c. Topography			
d. Degree of urbanization			
4. Politics			
a. Stable government			
b. Business friendly			
5. Sociology			
a. Religion			
b. Ethnic issues			
c. Gap between rich and poor			
6. Demographics			
a. Age			
b. Occupation			
c. Rate of home ownership			
d. Number of urban dwellers			

WORKSHEET 1—CONTINUED

Evaluation Criteria	Country A	Country B	Country C
7. Lifestyle			
a. Affluence			
b. Amount of leisure time			
8. Purchasing habits			
a. Brand loyalty			
b. Country loyalty			
9. Competition			
a. Direct			
b. Indirect			
10. Regulatory issues			
a. Laws and regulations			
b. Testing requirements			
11. Ease of access			
a. Travel time			
b. Travel costs			
c. Visit frequency			
12. Product redesign			
a. Electrical changes			
b. Overall redesign			
c. Labelling			
d. Packaging			

8
MARKET-ENTRY PLANNING

Your market-entry plan determines how you will approach the target export market. It should also include a schedule and estimates of what entering the export market will cost.

1. Initial Market-Entry Activity

Your entry into a particular export market will probably involve two activities: identifying and establishing yourself with a local agent; and doing what you can to promote your product. Chapter 10, Retaining an Agent, provides information on how to retain an agent, but at this stage you will only want to estimate how you will do this and what it will cost. Similarly, Chapter 11, Promoting Your Product, provides information on how to develop a promotion strategy, but at this stage you only want to make some approximations about the schedule and the cost.

There are several ways to meet potential agents, and the Canadian International Trade Centres should be able to help you with the following:

♦ Putting you in contact with the Canadian embassy trade officials responsible for your product in the target country, and having them provide you with a list of potential agents that you can contact. In order to decide which agent to work with, you will have to eventually meet with the agents you short list.

♦ Including you in an outgoing mission of Canadian companies similar to the target market. These missions are hosted by the local Canadian embassies who arrange for local agents and possible customers to meet with the Canadian business people. You have to pay your costs, but the contacts are arranged for you.

♦ Including you in a Canadian government-sponsored booth at a suitable trade show in the target country or region. You will have to pay most of your expenses, but government employees look after all the details.

You can also personally select a suitable trade show at which to exhibit your product and attract potential agents. Trade shows have become prolific in recent years so you must be careful about which one you choose. When you are looking for a trade show, always keep in mind your target audience. Ask yourself if they will attend the show and, if so, whether they will attend in sufficient numbers. For example, if your product is bathroom fixtures, you will probably have potential customers and agents visit your booth at a consumer home show. However, you will probably get more quality visits to a booth at a plumbing supply show.

For your initial visit, either to meet with agents or to exhibit at a trade show, you can probably use the same promotional material that you use with your Canadian customers. However, if you do not have a suitable brochure, you will have to produce one. Do not worry about producing a brochure in the local language at this early stage unless you are sure of your target audience and the translator. English brochures are acceptable because most agents are English-speaking or have somebody on their staff to help them translate, if required.

No matter what approach you take as your initial market-entry thrust, it will probably involve a visit to the target country, and this will probably be the first of many visits. So plan ahead and budget accordingly.

2. Marketing Plan and Schedule

The first activity you have to plan and schedule is the selection of an agent. The process of selecting an agent is explained in Chapter 10. Table 2 suggests the time you will need for each activity.

TABLE 2
AGENT SELECTION TIMETABLE

Identifying potential agents	4 months
Interviewing and selecting an agent	1 month
Negotiating an agent agreement	1 month

If your agent selection process involves exhibiting at a trade show, or even if you want to do a trade show just to introduce your product to the area, you will have to schedule a considerable amount of time for this activity. Unfortunately, you have no control over trade show dates, but they are usually planned well in advance. You will have to book a booth several months in advance, and you should take your time in preparing for the show, particularly if you are going to use new promotional material at your display booth. Table 3 suggests the time you will need for each activity.

TABLE 3
TRADE SHOW TIMETABLE

Select and book the trade show	6 months before the show
Design the show booth	3 months before the show
Prepare artwork and promotional material	2 months before the show
Ship trade show booth	2 weeks before the show

You should prepare a video of your product, both to show at the trade show and to leave with your agent. Videos vary tremendously in production time, cost, and quality. Even a basic video can take a few months to produce, and can cost $10 000 and up.

If you also have to produce a suitable brochure for the trade show or visit, you must allow time to do so, particularly if you have it done outside your company. If you decide to produce the brochure in the local language, you should also allow time to validate the translation. It is best if this is done by someone from the target country, because widely used languages such as Spanish and Arabic can differ from country to country. Allow the times suggested in Table 4.

TABLE 4
BROCHURE TIMETABLE

Layout and artwork	3 weeks
Translation (if required)	2 weeks
Validation of translation	1 month
Printing	2 weeks

Travel arrangements should also be made with a time schedule in mind, especially for the purposes of getting the required documentation. Table 5 suggests an effective schedule. Canadian passports can be obtained quite quickly but, to be safe, allow a few weeks. If you require a visa to visit the target country, allow plenty of time to obtain it. Countries such as Saudi Arabia can take several weeks to issue a visa. As well, if you are travelling with demonstration equipment, or even the trade booth itself, you will require documentation such as a carnet. This takes time to arrange. Last but not least, allow plenty of time for arrangements such as flight and hotel reservations. Travel in and out of a country may be booked up well in advance for festivals, religious holidays, and the like.

TABLE 5
TRAVEL ARRANGEMENT TIMETABLE

Apply for passport	3 weeks
Apply for visa	4 weeks
Obtain carnet	3 weeks
Make flight and hotel reservations	3 weeks

3. Marketing Costs

International marketing costs can be unexpectedly high, depending on the target country. Japan is probably the most expensive to visit, followed by some European countries. Table 6 shows some budgetary estimates of amounts you might be expected to pay for a market-entry visit to a country such as Germany.

TABLE 6
BUDGETARY MARKET ENTRY COSTS

Trade show		
	Space rental	$2 500
	Design	$1 500
	Artwork	$1 500
	Shipping	$2 500
	Subtotal	$8 000
Brochure		
	Layout & artwork	$1 500
	Translation	$1 000
	Printing	$2 000
	Video	$10 000+
	Subtotal	$14 500+
Travel		
	Airfare	$4 500
	Hotel for 5 nights	$1 200
	Local travel (car rental)	$700
	Living expenses for five days	$600
Subtotal		**$7 000**
TOTAL		**$29 500**

4. Cost and Schedule Planning

Your marketing plan should cover at least two years, because that could be how long it will take to get your first order, and you should budget accordingly. Table 7 shows a typical cost and marketing schedule over a two-year period. You might even want to fine-tune your schedule further by using months instead of quarters.

TABLE 7
TYPICAL MARKET ENTRY SCHEDULE AND COST ($)

Activity	[———Year One———]				[———Year Two———]			
	Q1	Q2	Q3	Q4	Q1	Q2	Q3	Q4
Trade show space rent	2 500							
Trade booth	3 000							
Shipping	2 500							
Brochure	4 500							
Video	10 000							
Trade show visit (2 person)		12 600						
Follow-up visit (1 person)				7 000				
Follow-up trade show						17 600		
Follow-up visit								7 000
Totals	22 500	12 600		7 000		17 600		7 000
Cumulative cost	22 500	35 100		42 100		59 700		66 700

5. Market-Entry Decision and Commitment

Now that you have done some planning and estimated the cost of market entry into a particular country, you are in a better position to make decisions. Your first inclination will be to try to trim the costs. Don't fool yourself into thinking you can enter an export market less expensively. You may be able to get away without a video, and that can save you quite a lot. You also may be able to scrimp a bit on the booth and brochure designs. But, all in all, your initial estimate is probably quite close to what your costs will be.

Of course, your big decision is, "Is it worth it?" To answer this question you will have to look at the possible sales you can expect — not the initial sales, but the sales over a longer period of time. Remember, exporting is a long-term activity. If the sales look as though they will pay for the marketing activity plus generate a reasonable profit, then you're on your way.

Before you get started on your initial marketing activity, however, make sure you have the company commitment for the long haul. You will have to be clear about how long it will take to get the first sales, and what it will cost to get to that stage. It is vitally important that the company be prepared to pay the cost. It is very bad business to begin an exporting venture and then have to terminate it for lack of funding. This is why you must spend the time doing comprehensive market-entry planning and budgeting.

6. Additional Information

The following sources of information about market-entry planning are available.

1. *Marketing Your Product.* Donald Cyr and Douglas Gray. Self-Counsel Press, 1998.

2. *Marketing Your Service.* Jean Withers and Carol Vipperman. Self-Counsel Press, 1998.

9
MAKING YOUR FIRST COUNTRY VISIT

Your first visit to a foreign country can be a bewildering experience, especially if the country has a distinctly different culture and language. However, if you are going to get into the export business, you will have to make these trips. This chapter should help answer many of the questions you have now, as well as the questions that arise when you get to where you are going. Checklist 2, which you will find later in this chapter, the Country Visit Checklist, includes the basic requirements for a business trip abroad, organized according to a time line.

1. Plan Ahead

There is no better way to gauge a foreign market than to investigate it "on the ground" during a personal visit. Once there, you have a chance to talk to potential customers, interview agents or distributors, and solidify relations with Canadian trade officials in the country. Your visit will also provide you with an opportunity to promote your product, your company, and yourself.

Many people believe that the first thing they have to do before visiting a foreign country is learn the language. This is definitely not true, particularly in business. English is rapidly becoming the international language of commerce today. Potential agents, and possibly customers as well, may not be fluent in English, but they will probably understand it in varying degrees. They will also have access to someone who understands the language quite well. Of course, if you take the time to learn a few phrases like "Hello" or "How are you?" in the native tongue, it will be appreciated and help break the ice among strangers.

It is more important to learn about the country you are visiting — its history, form of government, predominant religions, and culture. Most of this information is easy to find in a travel guide, or in the US Central Intelligence Agency's *World Fact Book*, available on the Internet at <www.odci.gov/cia/publications/factbook>. This information will give you insight into the business customs of the country. Saudi Arabia provides an example of why you should know about the country in order to do business there. In the 18th century, the Saud family aligned itself with the Wahabi religious movement, and together they assembled what is now the country of Saudi Arabia. This explains why religion continues to play a dominant role in every aspect of Saudi life. It also explains the power of the monarchy, and explains why you should try to get an agent with connections to key figures in the royal family.

Knowledge of the country's cultural makeup will also help you understand some of the local customs. For example, it may be important to be familiar with the Japanese custom of bowing and the significance of how deep the bow is. As in some other cultures, including Thailand, they prefer not to use the handshake. In Thailand, they prefer the "wai" gesture of bringing both palms together with a slight bow of the head to greet others. Also, in Thailand, it is rude to sit with your legs crossed and the sole of your foot pointing toward somebody.

Try to familiarize yourself with local gestures and practices before your departure, and use them in the appropriate context. While they may seem trivial to you, they could play a significant role in your relations with your foreign customers and business associates.

2. What to Take

Checklist 2, the Country Visit Checklist, includes the basic requirements for a business trip abroad, organized according to a time line. Here are a few additional tips about money and other personal items that you may want to take with you.

2.1 Traveller's cheques

Don't bother to get traveller's cheques in the currency of the country you are planning to visit. Take traveller's cheques in US dollars, which are the standard hard currency around the world. You can exchange them for the local currency at the standard rate when you have to, and often you can make purchases directly in US dollars or US traveller's cheques.

2.2 Currency exchange

Almost all international airports have currency exchanges where you can obtain the local currency. Unfortunately they are not always open when your flight arrives or departs. Take a few dollars' worth of the local currency with you from Canada to pay for the taxi to your hotel and other immediate expenses. You can get currency for most countries at the foreign exchange counter of any major Canadian bank, or from commercial money exchanges.

2.3 Credit cards

Major credit cards are accepted all over the world, and it is a good idea to take a variety of them with you. By using your cards you eliminate the need for carrying large amounts of traveller's cheques or cash.

2.4 Emergency food

Consider carrying a few energy food bars with you. These are an excellent safeguard against going hungry if your flight arrives after all the local restaurants have closed for the night, or if you don't have time to eat before your first meeting. Energy bars are usually equal to the nutritional value of a meal, and are available at most drugstores, health-food stores, and travel outfitters.

CHECKLIST 2
COUNTRY-VISIT CHECKLIST

1. Several months before your trip

Have you:

❑ Begun background reading on the country or countries you will be visiting?

❑ Begun obtaining information about suitable candidates, if one of the reasons for the trip is to select an agent?

❑ Checked your passport to ensure that it is up to date and will not expire during your trip? If required, have you applied for a new passport?

❑ Checked the visa requirements of the country you plan to visit, and started making arrangements to obtain one if required?

❑ Identified which immunizations (if any) you will require both to enter the country or countries you plan to visit and to re-enter Canada?

❑ Made your travel arrangements (flights and hotels), and checked to ensure that you are not going to arrive during a holiday, festival, or religious celebration?

2. Several weeks before your trip

Have you:

❑ Reviewed your promotional literature and identified what you will take, whether you need translation services, and so on?

❑ Checked your business cards to ensure that you have enough for the trip? Considered having them translated into the language of the country, with English on one side and the local language on the other side?

❑ Reviewed your product samples and demonstration equipment to ensure that you have the latest versions and that they are working correctly?

❑ Obtained a carnet for any demonstration equipment you plan to take with you, if applicable (see Appendix E)?

3. Several days before your trip, you should begin setting aside items you will take.

Have you included:

❑ Information about the country?

CHECKLIST 2—CONTINUED

❏ Promotional literature?

❏ Business cards?

❏ Samples and/or demonstration equipment?

❏ Carnet?

❏ Passport?

❏ Visas?

❏ International Certificate of Vaccination?

❏ Medication for stomach upset, diarrhea, malaria, and other health problems?

❏ Traveller's cheques?

❏ Currency of the country?

❏ Small gifts for local contacts, possible agents, and customers?

Also be sure to confirm all travel arrangements (flights and hotels) at this time.

2.5 Dress

Check on the recommended dress for westerners and pack accordingly. Business suits are usually acceptable for both men and women anywhere in the world, but you may want to take additional lightweight shirts or blouses for hot climates. In some countries with high temperatures and humidity, such as Singapore and Thailand, you will need to change your clothing several times a day. Never try to emulate the dress of the local population.

2.6 Luggage

Don't overburden yourself with luggage. Remember that most hotels offer laundry and dry-cleaning services. You might also want to courier extra brochures and videos to your hotel, rather than carry them in your luggage. Do make sure you take some with you, though, in case the couriered packages are lost.

3. Travel Documents

1. *Passport:* Be sure to have all the required travel documents in hand well before you leave on your trip, including a valid passport. If you already have a passport, check its expiry date — many a trip has been delayed while a passport was being renewed.

2. *Entry visa:* Some countries require an entry visa, and others require an exit visa as well. Consult the country's embassy or consulate for information about what you will need and how to obtain it. You will probably have to pay to get the visa. Some countries have different kinds of visas and separate rules and stipulations for each. For example, a "business" visa for some South American countries may require you to pay income tax while you are in the country.

3. *International certificate of vaccination:* If you are travelling to a country where medical problems are prevalent, you may have to obtain an international certificate of vaccination. This document is a small booklet about the size of a passport. It contains the dates of vaccinations you have taken for yellow fever, cholera, polio, and other diseases. It can usually be obtained from your doctor when you go for your first shot. The certificate is not necessarily required for entry into the country with the problem, but you may have to show it before entering other countries (including Canada) once you have made your visit.

   You should also arrange to have health insurance for travelling outside Canada. You can buy short-term travel medical insurance at travel agencies, banks, and many other outlets. If you frequently travel outside Canada, it is wise to obtain annual travel insurance that covers you whenever you travel. If you have any permanent medical conditions, you might also want to check the insurance policy to see if you are covered for the precondition.

4. *Customs forms and international carnets:* If you are going to carry equipment or samples with you, you will need suitable customs forms to take them across borders, and also to bring them back into Canada without paying duty on them. Under the NAFTA agreement, you can temporarily import certain goods duty-free into the United States and Mexico. Goods

that qualify include "professional equipment (tools of the trade), equipment for the press or for radio or television broadcasters, cinematographic equipment, goods for sports purposes, and goods for display or demonstration" (see Chapter 13). For most other countries, you should obtain an international carnet (pronounced "car-nay"). This document allows you to import and export items temporarily without paying duty on them. The carnet is fully explained in Appendix E.

4. Travel Arrangements

When planning your trip, try to allow as much time as possible in each country. A good rule of thumb is to stay no fewer than three days per stop, and to visit no more than three countries in two weeks. Also, give yourself some time to acclimatize and overcome jet lag. If it's a long trip, try not to schedule any meetings on the day you arrive. If you are travelling across many time zones, as you would on a trip to the Middle East or Asia, you might want to break up the trip by spending a day in one place somewhere along the way.

Arrange your flights carefully on the assumption that you will not be able to make changes once you arrive at your destination. In many countries, travel agents work for only one airline and, even if there is more than one airline, there may be no alternate flights available. If possible, contact your own travel agent back home and have them make the changes for you, or make your own changes via the Internet on your laptop computer. Also ensure that you are booked on a reliable airline. Airline safety and schedule considerations are not the same the world over.

Local travel can be a problem until you have made arrangements with a local agent, who will usually take you around. On your own you, will have to rely on taxis. Unfortunately, in many countries you cannot simply telephone a taxi and ask to be picked up. The safest taxis are those connected with the hotel you are visiting. Often it is a good idea to hire a taxi by the hour, and have the driver wait while you conduct your business meeting. At least then you are assured of a ride back to your hotel.

5. Appointments

When planning your trip, check the dates of local holidays in the country. You don't want to arrive just before a two- or three-day festival period, when most businesses are closed. Also find out about the weekends in the country, as they are not the same all over the world. In most Arab countries the weekend is Thursday and Friday, with Friday being their holy day. In Israel the weekend is Friday and Saturday; in Pakistan it is Friday and Sunday.

You may find it difficult to schedule exact meeting times with customers before your trip. Even your agent will be reluctant to set up appointments until you arrive. Many business people frequently change their travel plans and may not arrive in the country in time for a meeting arranged several weeks earlier. The locals have been stung too many times, so they often wait to set a meeting time after you have arrived in the country.

Punctuality is not a universally respected practice, sometimes with good reason. For example, it is almost impossible to judge how long it will take to get anywhere in Bangkok because of the legendary traffic jams. Appointment times are often assumed to be approximate, and you may have to wait for hours to meet your contact. Do not schedule your appointments too close together.

Don't be annoyed if you experience interruptions during your meeting with a local business person in his or her office. These interruptions are common practice in many countries, and are no indication of disinterest in you. They might even give you a better understanding of how important the person is, how he or she fits into the organization, and how the business runs.

Another potential annoyance is a last-minute change or cancellation of a meeting. This may be caused by somebody of higher influence convincing the person to meet urgently with him or her, and you unfortunately get bumped. However, there will be times when you get an urgent meeting because your agent was able to have somebody else bumped.

6. Personal Safety

When you are travelling overseas on business you face a number of personal safety risks that range from health risks to the risk of financial loss.

6.1 Travel-related diseases

The following discussion relates to travel-related diseases and how to reduce the risks of contracting them.

1. *Diarrhea:* Depending on the country you are visiting, unsanitary conditions can be a serious hazard to your health. "Don't drink the water," as the old joke goes, is actually good advice. Diarrhea is the most frequent illness to strike international travellers. It has many causes, but one of the most common is water-borne viral or bacterial infections. Uncooked foods such as fruits and salads are another source, so it is best to avoid eating any raw vegetables or fruits that do not have a protective skin (such as bananas or oranges) that you peel yourself. To be safe you should always carry medication, such as Imodium, to counteract diarrhea.

2. *Malaria:* If you will be travelling to a tropical climate, check with your local health authorities to see if you should guard against malaria. The usual preventive treatment involves taking quinine-based pills a few weeks before, during, and a few weeks after your trip. However, newer strains of malaria that are resistant to quinine have evolved, so you may have to take more potent measures. Your local health authorities will be able to advise you.

3. *Hepatitis and* HIV: Another frightening thought for the international traveller is that 80 percent or 90 percent of the blood supply in some countries is contaminated with hepatitis or HIV. There is not much you can do about this if you get into a serious accident, other than to avoid a blood transfusion if at all possible. Excellent information about preventing blood transfusions is available through the Blood Care Foundation Web site at <www.bloodcare.org.uk/bcf_html/traveller .html#solutions>.

6.2 Credit cards

Your credit cards, airline tickets, and certainly your money are very attractive to thieves. Always carry a list of your credit card numbers with you in a separate location from the cards, so you can easily cancel them in the event that they are stolen. A simple way of doing this is to photocopy your cards, as well as the front pages of your passport. Carry the photocopies in your suitcase and briefcase, and also leave copies at your office or home.

6.3 If your identification is stolen

You should have some additional suitable identification with you besides your passport, in case it is lost or stolen. In some countries you will have to surrender your passport to local authorities and hotels. There is usually no problem, but on occasion it can get "misplaced." If you have alternate identification, you can easily get assistance from the Canadian embassy staff.

6.4 Your itinerary

Make a complete itinerary of your trip and leave a copy of it with someone at home. Provide the Canadian embassy with a copy of it as well, particularly if the region is experiencing unrest. The embassy staff can advise you about any travel problems, and help you if a crisis arises.

6.5 Assault and terrorism

Finally, assault and terrorism are genuine threats to travellers in many parts of the world. You are best advised to maintain a low profile in your travels. If your business happens to be with the military or government, avoid broadcasting the fact with stickers or symbols emblazoned on your luggage or briefcase. Don't be overly paranoid, but be suspicious of anyone who approaches you.

7. Additional Information

The Internet has a wealth of information about making your first country visit. The following Web site is well worth exploring and bookmarking for future use.

1. US Central Intelligence Agency *World Fact Book*.
    Available through their Web site at
    <www.odci.gov/cia/publications/factbook>.

10
RETAINING AN AGENT

This chapter provides information about selecting an agent to represent your products in a target market. It includes a description of what an agent can do for you, different types of agents, what to look for in a potential agent, and agent contracts. It also discusses the importance of establishing a sound agent relationship.

1. Why You Need an Agent

Many business people hold the mistaken belief that business throughout the world is conducted the same way it is at home. However, once they take the first steps in exporting, they realize they need the local knowledge and connections of an in-country agent. Agents are a basic requirement of the business. Regardless of the size of the company or nature of the product, it still needs a link to the local community.

A good agent provides this link, as well as other services. He can help you deal with the local language, laws, customs, and often confusing business practices. However, the agent's first and most important function is to identify customers for your product, and market it to these customers. Local customers and end users may be different from those in Canada, and can only be identified by someone who is familiar with the target market and the various potential applications of your product within that community.

An agent's customers and connections should match your product as much as possible. For example, in-country agents who deal with buyers from supermarket chains will probably be highly successful selling your product if you are marketing a food item. However, if you are marketing a product more suited to the fishing industry, you need to find an agent well connected to the fishing industry. The agent's connections are very important to you, because with good, suitable connections, he can quickly get your product into the market.

A good agent can also uncover other opportunities for you. As the agent becomes more familiar with your product, he is better able to see potential local applications in slightly modified form, and to identify those who might want it. If, for example, your company manufactures a security system that is used in airports to detect passengers with hidden weapons, a good agent might identify other applications, such as use in banks. The agent could open a whole new market segment for you.

Agents also bridge the language and culture barriers you encounter in your exporting business. All agents have to speak English, or they would not be in business for long. You do not have to learn a country's language to do business in that country, although, as mentioned earlier, learning a few words, such as common greetings, is much appreciated by the locals. Agents can also help you understand and abide by local cultural differences, but make sure you learn as much about them as you can before your first country visit.

Agents normally translate for you, acting as interpreters in any meetings you have with customers who do not speak English. During these meetings, be prepared to sit for long periods while the discussion proceeds around you without your participation. However, watch what you do say when asked a question, because the customers may understand more English than they have led you to believe. It is not uncommon to give a sales pitch through an agent interpreter, only to discover during a subsequent meeting that the customer understands much of what you say before it is translated.

Agents can also help you validate translations of your brochures, videos, and other marketing literature. This is particularly important if you are dealing in a language such as Spanish or Arabic that is used in many countries, because some words have different meanings in different countries. For example, a Venezuelan-born Spanish translator once translated the cover of a sonar transducer into a Spanish word that was common slang for a condom in Mexico. Be sure that your agent verifies the name and descriptive label you are giving a product. It could have a totally different meaning in the target country.

Agents can help you with your local travel and living arrangements better than any Canadian travel agent. They can suggest hotels that are more convenient and better priced, and can usually help you out with local transportation as well.

Agents are your main communication link to your customers in the target country. In most cases all you have to do is make your proposal or quote in English to the agent, and he will translate it into the local language. You will have to provide additional artwork such as diagrams and pictures, which your agent will include in the non-English version. He will also ensure that the format is locally acceptable, which can be very important if you are making a proposal to a government customer. There is always the question of how accurate the translation is, but you can do little about this. The agent will deliver the proposal or documentation to the correct person in the customer organization and, in some cases, will also provide copies to other interested and influential parties.

Local government regulations and controls in some countries can be very confusing. It is part of the agent's job to be familiar with the regulations and ways to work within them or, in some cases, to work around them. A simple, yet important, example of this is obtaining an entry visa into the country. A good agent not only provides the required paperwork, such as a letter of invitation, but also is able to expedite the visa approval.

An agent can help you with many other regulations and controls. In some countries, certain products must undergo lengthy testing before they are approved for sale (much like Canadian Standards Association testing). An agent can monitor and assist in this process and, as is often required, an agent will take steps to expedite it.

In some countries, particularly in the Middle East and South America, the law requires that a local agent represent you. In a few of these countries the law can also bind you to the agent for life. This can have a significant effect on your business in the country if you initially choose the wrong agent. Even if the agent does nothing for you and you switch to a more useful agent, you will still have to pay commissions to the first agent. When researching the country, make sure you investigate the marketing agent legal requirements and laws in general. The Canadian embassy should be able to help you in this regard.

2. Types of Agents

There are several types of local marketing agents. The type of agent you choose, and the business arrangement you make with him, will depend to a large extent on the nature of your product and the types of customers you anticipate. Before you begin your search for an agent, you must decide what you want him to do for you. To help you in this decision, this section outlines the most common types of agents and their modes of operation.

You should also be aware of the possibility of needing more than one agent in a country. This can happen when a company has quite different products or customer profiles. Agents usually concentrate on the products and customers with which they are familiar, sometimes to the detriment of other client products or potential customers. Under these circumstances they are usually quite happy to let another agent handle the other products or customers. For example, you may arrange to have one agent distribute your product to local wholesalers and supermarkets, but contract with another to handle any business with the military. There is usually no legal problem in doing this as long as the products and the customers with which each agent deals are defined in the agent agreements.

2.1 Commissioned agents

The most common agent arrangement made by exporters, and the simplest, is that of a commissioned agent. The agent earns a commission on any sales that he makes for you, and only when the sale is made. The main advantage to this arrangement is that the agents have a very big incentive to sell for you. The more they sell, the more they make. The disadvantage is that if your products are harder to sell, or take more time than other product lines, the agent may not bother with them.

Commission rates vary from country to country, depending on how much effort the agent must make and on the overhead required to obtain a contract. Commissions can be as low as 3 percent or 4 percent or as high as 25 percent. They can also vary according to the sales volume. For example, the agent may get 10 percent for sales up to $100 000, 8 percent for sales between $100 000 and one million dollars, and 6 percent for everything over a million dollars.

2.2 Retainer agents

Retainer agents are paid a fixed amount to work for your company for a specific period of time. They are usually contracted on a yearly basis to work a stated number of days per year or month on your behalf, for a fixed fee or retainer.

There are two major disadvantages to this type of business relationship. First, retainer agents know they will get paid whether or not they accomplish anything for you. Since you are not usually in regular contact with them, it is difficult for you to ensure that they are actually doing the work. Resulting sales are one indication of their effectiveness, but perhaps they could have gotten even more business for you. This is the second disadvantage: they have no incentive to get additional business by expending just a bit more effort. They are paid the same amount no matter how much business they generate for you.

The disadvantages do not mean that you should never use retainer agents. In some countries this is the only type of agent available. Most agents do not take advantage of the situation because they want their contracts renewed.

2.3 Retainer or commissioned agents

There is a growing trend among exporters to pay agents a combination of fixed retainer and commission. This is especially true in military marketing because of the long time and effort involved in making a sale. Also, an agent's marketing expenses are sometimes higher than the commission rate, so the retainer augments the commission, ensuring that the agent's overhead is covered.

This type of arrangement represents the best of both worlds for agents. They get paid regularly whether they do anything or not, and when they make a sale they get a commission as well. However, most agents will still strive to get as much business for you as they can.

2.4 Multinational agents

Some agency companies act as local agents for a number of client companies in a number of countries. These companies usually specialize in a particular product line, such as medical or security equipment. Although the commissions or discounts they require may seem high, multinational agents can establish a very effective international marketing division for your company. This approach can save you a lot of money and effort, as you do not have to select, contract with, and work with a number of different agents in different countries.

You will also run into regional agents who work a number of countries in a region. For example, agents in Singapore often sell to Malaysia, Indonesia, Sri Lanka, and other neighbouring countries. This arrangement can be advantageous to you in that you have to deal with only one agent in the region. You must be aware of any political, religious, or ethnic frictions among the countries, however, because they may limit the agent's effectiveness.

2.5 Canadian-based agents

Canadian-based agents sell to other countries while operating from Canada. They are often foreign nationals who have been educated in Canada, and who operate a Canadian company that sells Canadian products to their homelands. Canadian-based agents usually work with local agents in their home countries. Using this type of agent can cut down on your communication problems, and you negotiate the contract with your agent under Canadian law. However, you should ensure that the agent's contacts in his home country are appropriate for your product, and that the agent can sell for you.

2.6 Distributors

A distributor is an agent who purchases your products from you and then resells them. Distributors can vary from little more than commissioned agents to agents who stock your products, including spare parts, and also do repair work on them. They make their money by buying the products at wholesale prices and marking them up as they see fit. Or they buy your product at a discount, the amount of which depends on the number of sales, and sell it at your listed price.

If you require distributors to service your products, you will have to carefully screen them to ensure that they have the technical capability to do so. You will also have to train their staff, and you may have to provide special tooling and so on. You will want to make sure that your distributor is financially secure and will be in business for a while.

Distributors can greatly affect your reputation and hence your business in a country. If they provide good service as well as sales, the word will soon spread and your business is likely to grow on the good reputation. But if they don't provide good service you will probably have few follow-on sales, and the business will dwindle.

2.7 Branch offices

A branch office is a part of your company in a foreign country. It can be staffed by your Canadian personnel, by locals, or, most often, by a combination of the two. It can even be a one-person operation, employing an individual you send to the country for a few years to develop the market. A potential problem with the branch office is that it is subject to the laws of the country in which it operates, and these laws can be quite daunting, particularly with regard to labour relations. The advantage of having a branch office is that your company has complete control over it, including how it markets and prices your products.

2.8 Contractor or subcontractor arrangements

For some products you may not want the traditional agent relationship; you may wish to simply act as a subcontractor to a local company that will include your product as part of its product. As an example of this arrangement, say that you provide sensors for a large security system that the local company sells. The local company is the prime contractor that is directly responsible to the customer, and puts together the complete system. You are the subcontractor to the local company: you provide the sensors, as well as installation service and training.

The type of company you select to work with will depend on the product. You will want to ensure that the company can handle the complete job before you make any commitment to them, because you don't want to end up doing more of the work than you contracted for. Some of the things you should check out are the technical capabilities of the company, its personnel resources, and certainly its financial stability.

2.9 Joint ventures

Joint ventures are set up by two or more companies to carry on a particular business or project. The founding companies jointly own the joint venture company, with the terms of ownership usually based on the percentages of their investments in the company. In return, the joint venture contracts portions of the business back to the founding companies. Joint ventures are a popular approach because they often include local in-country businesses in the joint venture. This can be advantageous to you as the exporter because you do not have to worry about the local laws, labour, or marketing. Your local joint venture partner usually looks after these aspects of the business. The disadvantage is that the local joint venture partner can sometimes use the local laws or government influence to push you out of the business once it is thriving. In China there is the additional problem that, at the end of the joint venture, all assets of the joint venture company revert to the Chinese partner, according to Chinese law.

2.10 Strategic partnering

Strategic partnering is used to create a presence in a relatively closed market. For example, you may want to set up a strategic partner arrangement with a company in France that will give you access to the European market. In return, your strategic partner has access to the North American market. The problem is to find a suitable partner. Ideally, your partner should be close enough to your business to enable reciprocal marketing efforts, but not so close to your product as to become a competitor to you in your own market.

3. Issues to Consider

The type of agent you select and the business arrangement you make with the agent will depend on both your product and a number of other factors. Use Worksheet 2, the Agent Type Worksheet, to help you evaluate some of the issues you should consider when deciding on your agent relationship.

WORKSHEET 2
AGENT TYPE WORKSHEET

Use the following questions to help you decide on your type of agent and business relationship.

1. Market considerations

    What is the best way to penetrate the market?

    Will your customers expect after-sales service?

    Is there potential follow-on business?

    Is it advantageous to be a foreign supplier?

2. Marketing costs

    Which business relationship provides the most efficient and least expensive market coverage?

    A commissioned agent is probably the least expensive, but is this approach effective for your product?

    If you require a distributor arrangement, would it be cost effective to open a branch office?

3. Proposals

    Will detailed proposals be required in the local language?

    If so, who will handle the translation?

    Can you propose a complete solution to the customer requirements, or will you have to involve another company or companies?

4. Technical knowledge

    Does the local representative require a high level of technical knowledge to handle your product?

    Is long-term training required? Does the agent have the appropriate staff to undertake the training?

5. Installation and support

    Who will do the installation?

    Who will provide follow-up support?

    What are the costs associated with these issues?

6. Legal considerations

   What kinds of business relationships are permitted under local laws?

   What other legal obligations are associated with each business relationship?

7. Business relationships

   How can you measure agent effectiveness?

   Can you easily switch to another agent if your first one does not work out?

   What are the costs of changing agents?

4. Identifying Potential Agents

Once you have decided on the type of agent you want in each country, your next step is to develop a list of suitable contenders for the job. The Canadian government can help you in this regard (see Chapter 6). Your nearest International Trade Centre will put you in contact with the trade officials in the Canadian embassy of the target country. Trade officials can usually send you a list of suitable agents, often including some information about each one. Select a number of these agents that appear to be right for you and contact them. In your initial letter or fax you can explain your interest in acquiring an agent, briefly describe your product, and ask them to provide more information about themselves. You might even prompt them by asking for the following information:

♦ What is the size of the agency in personnel and gross sales?

♦ What products do they specialize in?

♦ To whom do they sell?

♦ What are some of their recent achievements?

Sometimes interested agents learn about you through your advertising or your Internet site, if you have one. If the agency's initial letter or fax to you sounds plausible, reply and ask the questions listed above. If they are not a viable agency, your questions might scare them off. If they provide you with at least some of the requested information, you can decide whether you'd like further information.

At other times you may receive an unsolicited approach from an agent who is passing on genuine customer interest in your product. For example, the customer may have seen your product somewhere and would like to find out more about it. He approached an agent with the query, and the agent in turn contacts you. This can be very fortuitous for you, and you should respond to the opportunity as soon as possible.

Trade shows are an excellent means of identifying potential agents. Major trade shows in North America are attended by potential buyers and agents from around the world, so you may not have to go far to identify suitable agents. Similarly, agents from several countries usually attend trade shows in nearby countries. If you exhibit at a major trade show in a place such as Singapore, you will probably be visited by agents from Malaysia, Indonesia, India, and other neighbouring countries.

5. The Agent Selection Process

The amount of business you generate in a country will be a direct function of the agent you select, yet many companies pay little attention to the important process of agent selection. When you make your agent evaluations you should use a predetermined questionnaire. The questionnaire should also be used during agent interviews. It will add to your credibility in the eyes of the potential agents by demonstrating that you are serious about selecting an agent, and that you have already done some homework. By using a questionnaire you also cover all of the main issues, and you ensure that you evaluate each of the agent contenders on the same basis. Even a vague answer to a specific question can provide you with substantial information about the agent. Your questionnaire will vary depending on the type of agent or business relationship you desire. Worksheet 3 is a suggested agent questionnaire to help you.

Be prepared to spend a considerable length of time deciding on an agent, both during the visit to the country and on return to Canada. Do not make a hasty decision during a hurried schedule in a foreign country, because it is easy to miss what could be a critical aspect of a potential agent. Also, once you are back in Canada, you can talk to people in other companies who may be able to provide you with additional information about the country and the agent situation there.

WORKSHEET 3
AGENT QUESTIONNAIRE WORKSHEET

1. Company name or division_____

   _____

   (A smaller company may be a division of a much larger company, with access to the resources of its parent.)

2. Personnel contacted_____

   _____

   _____

   (The position of the person you deal with at the agency should be considered in your assessment. Marketing and sales people will judge your product on how easily they can sell it. Marketing managers will look at the larger picture to see how your product will fit in with their other product lines. Senior company people, such as presidents and managing directors, will tend to consider your business in terms of their overall business strategy.)

3. Specialization _____

   _____

   _____

   (Make sure the agent you select specializes in your type of products and deals with your potential customers. If you sell car radios, you will probably not get much business through an agent who sells to hospitals.)

4. Size _____

   _____

   _____

   (Success is not necessarily a function of the size of the agency. To move most consumer products you need an agency with many contacts, and this usually means a large company with branches throughout the country you are targeting. For highly specialized products aimed at specialized markets, however, it may be best to deal with a smaller agency that specializes in your target market.)

5. Ownership _____

   _____

   _____

   (Ownership of an agency may not seem important, but in some countries it can have a considerable impact on your business. For example, an agency owned by the pension fund of the country's armed forces would be very useful if you are selling military products.)

WORKSHEET 3—CONTINUED

6. Recent achievements _____
_____
_____

(An agency's recent achievements are a good indication of how effective it is, the type of customers it deals with, the products it handles, and the size of the projects it undertakes. Make sure that the achievements they tell you about are valid and not just marketing hype.)

7. Other representation _____
_____
_____

(The list of companies and products that an agency represents can indicate how effectively it will represent you. You want to try to find an agency that handles products that are of interest to your type of customer, but at the same time avoid dealing with someone who already handles products very similar to yours. Client lists do not have to be long to be impressive. There is quite a difference between an agency that handles a long list of small companies with obscure products, and one that represents a few well-known firms and products.)

8. Customer contacts _____
_____
_____

(In many countries, and for many products, an agent's contacts are more important than any other aspect of the operation.)

9. Aggressiveness_____
_____
_____

(Aggressiveness in an agency can be an important feature. There is no value in an agency that is not prepared to get out there and sell for you.)

10. Business arrangement _____
_____
_____

(Find out what kind of business arrangement the agency wants, such as commissioned agent or distributor, and make sure it is what you are looking for.)

You may decide to conduct your initial interviews in your hotel, but be sure to also visit the facilities of the agents you have on your short list. The visit will give you a much better feel for the company's size, specialties, and overall methods of doing business. It is also easier to speak with those in senior positions in the company during a personal visit. However, bear in mind that appearances can be deceiving, and that a very humble-looking operation may have excellent contacts for your business.

Gather as much documentation as possible on the agents you are evaluating, both during the agent interview or facility visit, and on return to your office. You might want to run a credit check on them through an agency such as Dun & Bradstreet. The Canadian embassy trade officials may also be able to help you by providing additional information about the agents they have obtained from other companies.

6. The Agent Contract

You will eventually have to negotiate some form of contract with an agent. Most will demand one before they do anything on your behalf. Others will not want a contract until they can test the market to determine whether they can sell your product. Instead they may ask for a letter of intent to ensure that you will give them a contract if they get some business for you. Obviously the second type of contract is preferable because it allows both parties to test the viability of your product in the market before making any commitment.

Agent contracts vary according to the type of business relationship, the product, and the proposed market. However, the following basic information is always included in any agency agreement:

1. Names of the contracting parties

   The names and addresses of the contracting companies are stated and, in most cases, a contact person in each company is named in the contract.

2. Date of the contract

   The exact date on which the contract is signed or begins is stated, because it usually determines the date on which it will be terminated.

3. Territory covered by the agent

   The specific area or territory in which the agent will represent your products is defined. Most agents want as much territory as they can get. However, it is better to authorize a smaller territory and see how they do. It can be expanded later if you both agree.

4. Products to be marketed

   You should be specific about which products you want the agent to market for you, especially if you are going to have other agents in the same territory marketing other products of yours.

5. Agent's responsibilities

   You should stipulate the main services that the agent is to perform for you. If he is to participate in trade shows or other promotions, you should also state who pays for what.

6. Exporter's responsibilities

   You should define what you will do to support the agent, such as providing brochures, samples, and demonstration equipment.

7. Agent's remuneration

   Terms of payment are undoubtedly of great interest to the agent, and the terms should be clearly defined. For example, if your agent sells strictly on commission, you may not want to pay him a percentage of the contract when you win it. You may instead want to pay your agent only when you get paid, even if this entails progress payments spread out over several years.

8. Duration of the contract

   The duration of the contract will depend on the product, because some products, such as military equipment, may take several years of marketing before a sales contract is won. Or you might have a one-year contract that is automatically renewable for as long as both parties agree to it, which would save you some paperwork and legal costs.

9. Termination options

   The agreement should allow for the termination of the contract by either side before the expiry date. The usual approach is to state that either party can terminate the contract by giving in writing to the other a specific number of days' warning.

10. Law governing the contract

The agreement should state under what laws its terms are enforceable, and the method the parties agree to use to settle disputes. Obviously, a contract under the laws of Canada is best for you, rather than under the laws of the agent's country. However, you may not be able to have it this way, if the agent law of the foreign country states that the agreement must be under its law.

There may be many other terms you want to write into your agent agreement or contract, depending on the nature of your business. The terms listed above are only basic suggestions. Always obtain legal advice when drawing up a contract such as this. To save time and money, you might want to develop a standard agency agreement that you can use with agents around the world.

7. The Agent Relationship

Agents service several foreign suppliers at once and thus require occasional motivation from you to keep your products at the top of their interest. The best way to motivate your agent is by maintaining regular contact and visiting the agent and his market as often as you can. The more help you give, the more your agent will give you in return.

Ensure that your agent has plenty of marketing material, such as brochures, videotapes, and company gifts. The first thing most agents ask for is a catalogue and price list. A catalogue can make life a lot easier for the agent, but a catalogue is in not much use for goods that are complex and customized. In this case all you can do is provide him with brochures and technical documentation, and hope that both the agent and the customer can understand them.

Each time you visit the market, try to have your agent arrange for you to brief potential customers on your product or reinforce previous exposure. These briefings are important to the agent as a means of developing a better relationship with the customer. The agent will also learn more about the product as he listens to your briefing.

In between visits to the market area, contact your agent regularly. Telephone or fax weekly either to ask for an update on a particular customer, or just to talk. You can discuss contracts you have won in other countries so your agent can incorporate the information into his marketing activity. You can also ask the agent for his input on new brochure designs and other promotional campaigns you are planning. All of this has the effect of making the agent feel more a part of your company, and it provides additional motivation for him to work on your behalf.

A good agent relationship often develops into a good personal relationship. Such a relationship in a foreign country gives you a rare opportunity to learn the local culture and customs, and to better understand your agent's approach to doing business. Accept invitations to visit your agent's home and to meet his family. You will soon realize that we are all really the same the world over — an attitude that is important to the success of your exporting business.

8. Additional Information

1. *Selecting and Using Foreign Agents and Distributors.* Department of Foreign Affairs and International Trade. Government of Canada, 1991.

11
PROMOTING YOUR PRODUCT

This chapter describes how to promote your product in the international market. It covers the various promotional alternatives available to you, including brochures, advertising, trade shows, and marketing support from the Canadian embassy.

Much has been written about how to promote a product (see the Additional Information section at the end of this chapter, which lists some of the resources available). This book will not go into all of the aspects of product promotion, but will address the sometimes subtle differences you should be aware of when you promote a product internationally.

1. International Promotion

Your international promotion campaign will depend on how you decide to enter the market. If you partner with a local company, you will probably rely on the promotional strategy it already has in place. In fact, this may be the reason you chose this partner in the beginning. If you use a distributor, your agreement may specify that the distributor is responsible for all promotion within the territory. If you contract with a commissioned agent, you will have to sort out who does what promotion activity, and who pays for it. And of course, if you decide to sell direct to the customer, you will be responsible for every aspect of your promotion strategy.

Promoting in a foreign market has many aspects similar to promoting in Canada. As in Canada, consumers in other industrialized countries have brand-name preferences, and new products are established only after they have competed successfully with those already in the marketplace. Niche marketing is also becoming widely practiced abroad, with producers targeting specific market segments and even customizing their products to accommodate a particular customer group. However, there are still significant differences between domestic and foreign promotion.

2. Developing an International Brochure

Your first promotional requirement is a suitable brochure. You simply cannot get away from the need for good product literature. You must always have something to leave with the customers and agents to remind them of your product. However, the brochure you use in an international market may be quite different from the one you currently use in Canada.

An international brochure should have plenty of colour photos and illustrations. The written commentary should focus on what the product does rather than how it does it. Descriptions should be simple, written in straightforward prose. Above all, do not use any idiomatic expressions that can be easily misinterpreted. Remember, the brochure's readers probably do not have English as their first language, so you want to make it as easy as you can for them. Also, customers and agents may translate the brochure into their own languages to explain it to others. You want to minimize any translation errors by making the language as simple as possible.

If you do translate the brochure into another language, make sure someone in the target country, such as your agent, validates the translation. Even though some languages such as Spanish and Arabic are common in several countries, the meanings for some words may vary from one country to the next. Remember the example in an earlier chapter of a Venezuelan translator using on the cover of electronic equipment a Spanish word that, in Mexico, was a slang word for condom.

If you do not want to produce a translated version of the brochure immediately, you can allow for it at a later date. An easy way to do this is to have only the brochure's colour artwork, including the photography, printed on several hundred or several thousand brochures. The colour work is the most expensive part of the production process, and is usually done before the written copy is printed over it anyway. Have the English copy printed on only a portion of the brochures, and keep the remainder for later when you have the translation ready. It is then just a simple matter of printing the foreign words over the previously printed artwork.

3. Advertising

Local media advertising is not recommended for exporters making their first move into a new target market, because it is fraught with questions and potential problems. Should you use newspapers? Billboards? Radio? Television? Who will pay for it? And how can you ensure that the ads are culturally attuned and worded according to colloquial usage? Your local agent can be of invaluable assistance to you in these matters.

Before you try any advertising in a new market area, learn something about the culture, traditions, and preferences of your target audience. If your product uses a logo, check to ensure that its colour and symbolism are in accordance with local tastes and sentiments. Colours, numbers, shapes, and certain non-verbal gestures incorporated into product labels should always be vetted by a local before they are distributed to a foreign audience.

Instead of local advertising, you might want to consider international magazines, particularly if your product appeals to a niche audience. Many international specialist magazines are sold throughout the world, with or without local translation. For example, *Jane's Defence Weekly*, which is based in the United Kingdom, is read by military people around the world. Many consumer magazines published in the United States are also distributed internationally. If you know of an international publication that your potential customers read regularly, explore the cost of advertising in it.

You will find that responses to your international advertising follow an interesting and predictable pattern. Your first responses will come from the customers you have been targeting. These are usually serious responses, and you should follow up immediately. You will also get some responses from would-be agents, to whom you may or may not want to reply. Then, as the magazine is read in institutional libraries, you will get inquiries from academics. These people probably have no intention of buying your product, but they may have useful connections that can be of help, so you may want to reply to them.

You should also consider arranging for articles about your product to be published in the same international magazines. Editors will often accept an article for publication if it is about a unique product or has a unique slant, is written in the style of the magazine, and has suitable pictures to accompany it. This can be a very cost-effective means of advertising.

4. Trade Shows

Trade shows are an excellent way to promote your product, testing the response to your product in a new market, and identifying potential agents. However, in recent years trade shows have become a product themselves, proliferating to such an extent that customers are very choosy about which ones they attend. It is important, therefore, that you research the value of a particular show before signing up for it. You want to be sure that the customers you are interested in will be attending in sufficient numbers to make your participation in the show worthwhile.

Since many shows held in the United States attract attendees from around the world, you may not have to go far to be assured of an international audience. Similar multi-national trade shows are held throughout Europe and Asia. For the most part, the international visitors are agents looking for products to sponsor in their homeland.

Once you have decided on an international trade show for your market entry, product promotion, or both, you should consider the following details.

4.1 What to exhibit

You have to first decide what product to exhibit, and how to exhibit it. Will you use the product itself as your primary display, or will you use a mock-up, or artwork only? Try to create an effective, eye-catching display or demonstration that identifies what your product is all about. Your exhibition should be product-based; avoid being simply flashy, such as having a belly dancer staff your booth. Remember, you want to attract customers, not just a crowd.

4.2 Booth type and size

Once you decide on what you will display and how you will display it, you then have to select the booth type and size. Size is usually a multiple of the standard nine-square-metre booth (100 square feet in the United States). Booths can be a separate island, on a corner, outside the display hall (usually for large products such as vehicles), or a chalet (a popular exhibit and entertainment space at air shows). Booths are usually allocated on a first-come, first-served basis. Companies that have been exhibiting at a particular show for several years often have priority over others in keeping their usual space and location. If you want a particular type of booth or location, you will have to book very early.

4.3 Artwork

No matter what you exhibit, you will need some artwork in your booth to explain your product or, at the very least, to show your company name. Don't forget that the artwork takes time to produce and, the bigger your booth, the more artwork you will need.

4.4 Literature

The trade show is where you can put your brochures to good use. You should also think of having more detailed information packages for visitors who show serious interest in your product and want more information. The packages might contain product specifications, a catalogue of other products, an annual report (or other descriptive document about the company), and, if appropriate, product samples.

4.5 Press kits

Prepare a number of press kits to give to the media when they drop by looking for material to write about. If members of the press do not come around to your booth, go find them yourself and give them a press kit. The press kit should have a brief magazine-style article about your product, some 20-by-25-centimetre (eight-by-ten-inch) glossy pictures suitable for reproduction, brochures, and other appropriate information.

When visitors drop by your booth, try to get as much information as possible from them. A business card is a good start, but you should also try to find out why they are at the trade show, and how that interest relates to your product. Do not be afraid to make notes in front of them. It shows that you are truly interested in what they are saying, and the notes are good reference for follow-up. And follow up you must: the connections you make are a key aspect of a trade show. Do not let the visitors you met forget your product. Be sure to contact them later to see if they are still interested.

Part of the difficulty in preparing for a trade show is remembering and meeting all of the deadlines. Checklist 3, at the end of this chapter, is a Trade Show Checklist that you can use as a reference.

5. Government-Supported Trade Shows

The Canadian government is an active participant in a number of trade shows around the world. Their usual approach is to rent a group of booths in an area of the trade show, called a trade booth complex. They then rent the booths out to Canadian companies who want to participate as part of the Canadian contingent. The government usually keeps a large booth for itself in the centre of the area, where it displays brochures from other Canadian companies. They also often host a meeting room with refreshments. Maple leaves abound, and the complex usually attracts considerable traffic at the show.

In addition to the trade booth complex, the local Canadian embassy often organizes meetings of local customers and agents at which the participating companies can give briefings or have one-on-one discussions. At times there is an embassy-sponsored cocktail party, to which the participating Canadian company staff are not only invited, but also encouraged to invite their potential customers. These added touches can be very helpful in establishing contacts in the country.

As well as reducing your costs and providing a means of establishing business relations, government-sponsored trade shows save you a great deal of organizational time. You are among other Canadians on whom you can rely if required. Also, because you are appearing under the banner of the Canadian government, your customers are assured that you have the government's blessing and support. To learn more about government-sponsored trade shows, contact your nearest International Trade Centre.

6. Government-Sponsored Trade Missions

As previously mentioned, the Canadian government and some provincial governments sponsor trade missions to foreign markets. The missions are usually organized around a particular business sector or industry, such as building products. Companies sign up for the mission, and their representatives travel together and participate in briefings and meetings with foreign customers that the local embassy has arranged. The companies usually pay their own expenses, but the government does all the organizing and sets up the customer contacts.

Both levels of government also sponsor incoming missions of foreign buyers and agents from a particular market area, such as China. The visiting group is usually taken to several Canadian cities, where they meet with appropriate Canadian company representatives. The government provides the meeting venue and, if required, the interpreters.

For more information on government-sponsored trade missions, contact your nearest International Trade Centre or your provincial government trade officials. See Appendix C for provincial trade office addresses.

7. Canadian Embassy Marketing Support

Trade officials in Canadian embassies around the world promote Canadian products and companies. They can be a great asset to you in a foreign country and are good people for you to work with. Trade officials can put you in touch with potential agents and customers such as government buyers, and can provide information on local companies. They can also distribute your brochures to local business people who visit the embassy. You might even get invited to cocktail or dinner parties at the embassy to meet some of the locals, or be invited to attend one of their staff parties like the TAIW party in Riyadh, Saudi Arabia. (TAIW is Thank Allah Its Wednesday, since the Muslim weekend is Friday and Saturday.)

To take advantage of embassy services, provide the senior trade official with information about your product, your company, and your plans for the local market. He or she will pass the information to the commercial staff person who looks after your product area, who will then contact you. You may be pleasantly surprised at the interest and support you get. The *Directory of Canadian Trade Commissioner Service*, published by the Canadian Department of Foreign Affairs and International Trade, lists the commercial staff in each Canadian embassy. However, this publication is often out of date because the staff are rotated fairly frequently.

There are limits to the senior trade official's time and to the services his or her department can provide. Remember, they are looking after many Canadian companies, large and small. Make sure your requests to them are reasonable. Table 8 lists what the Canadian embassy can and cannot do for you.

8. Customer Briefings and Seminars

Customer briefings are usually a key factor in a foreign market. Customer briefings can be group briefings, but more often they are one-on-one meetings in which you give your standard pitch to one or two people. The briefings are usually set up by your agent, who will also act as your interpreter if required. As mentioned earlier, these briefings are also good for the agent to get to know your product.

Seminars on your product can be a useful marketing tool, provided that your product lends itself to this kind of promotion. The seminars can be as short as a few hours or as long as a few days. The usual procedure is for your agent to send out faxes to the companies of potential customers to encourage their staff to attend the seminar at the announced time and place. The offer of refreshments is sure to increase attendance.

TABLE 8
CANADIAN EMBASSY TRADE SERVICES

The following is a list of services the Canadian embassy trade officials can and cannot provide for you.

CAN	CANNOT
• Promote your products or services in the local market	• Make actual sales for you
• Help you find a suitable agent	• Serve as your agent
• Stay in contact with your company representatives, inform them of potential avenues for your goods, and generally provide support	• Train your staff
• Find translators or interpreters for you	• Serve as your interpreter
• Provide you with information on local debt collection agencies	• Collect overdue bills
• Keep you informed of any changes in the political or social conditions in your target market that might affect your business or travel in the area	• Make travel arrangements for you

When the agent is setting up briefings and seminars, make sure that he or she also arranges for all of the support equipment you will need. Do not depend on the availability of the briefing equipment you take for granted back home. Computer projectors are still not that popular around the world, and 35 mm slide projectors are seldom available. The best solution is to use overhead projector slides. Many hotels and even companies have these projectors available, or you can rent one locally. If you take any of your own equipment, such as a small television and video player, make sure it is compatible with the local electrical supply.

Above all, make sure that you have a sufficient number of briefing or seminar handouts to leave with the attendees. The documentation you leave will enable them to contact you or your agent for additional information, or hopefully an order. Your handouts can range from a standard brochure to a package of technical data and even a video. You must have something to leave with the attendees so that you don't fall victim to the old adage, "Out of sight, out of mind."

9. Concept Proposals

If your product is relatively sophisticated, or has to be customized for the application, it is often a good idea to provide an interested customer with a concept proposal. Quite often, the customer cannot see exactly how the product will solve his or her problem. If you explain it to him or her in a short proposal aimed directly at the specific situation, it will be of great help. For example, it is often difficult for a customer to grasp how an integrated security system will work to protect the property it surrounds. You can help the customer understand the security system if you draw up a brief concept proposal of how the various components of the system could be located and operated. Include some sketches as well. The concept proposal does not have to be entirely accurate, but it must be clear enough to give the customer an idea of what he or she might need. Your objective, of course, is to be invited for more focussed discussions with the customer, leading to a more detailed proposal and, eventually, a contract.

10. After-Sales Service

While it is not usually part of your market-entry plan, after-sales service is important even at the market-entry stage. This is what often brings the customers back to you. Without reasonable after-sales service, your company and product image can badly suffer.

The contract with a foreign distributor should include the requirement for a stock of replacement parts and after-sales service. The extent of the service is usually detailed in the contract. You will have to provide the distributor with the parts, instruction manuals, and possibly training as well. These details must all be established when you negotiate the agency contract.

CHECKLIST 3
TRADE SHOW CHECKLIST

1. Six months before

❑ Review literature about the trade shows in which you are interested, including previous years' attendance, costs, space available, and deadlines.

❑ Identify the products you want to exhibit.

❑ Consider how you will exhibit the product or products, and begin planning the display.

❑ Decide on the trade show you want to attend, and make the application.

2. Three months before

❑ Review your promotional material and reorder as required.

❑ Finalize the booth design and begin production of it.

❑ Decide what staff you will have in the booth.

❑ Identify other marketing activities you may want to do while in the area.

❑ Make travel and accommodation arrangements for you and your booth staff.

❑ Apply for visas, if required.

❑ Identify the Canadian trade officials in the region and contact them.

❑ Investigate shipping issues, including customs regulations on the temporary import of the display equipment and the documentation required, and begin the paperwork?

❑ Arrange immunizations, if required.

3. One month before

❑ Complete shipping arrangements.

❑ Check your own and your booth staff's passports.

❑ Train staff for the booth.

❑ Send out invitations to potential customers and agents.

❑ Prepare information packages and press packages.

CHECKLIST 3—CONTINUED

4. One week before

❑ Check travel and accommodation arrangements.

❑ Recheck travel documents such as passports and visas.

❑ Check shipping progress of booth and display equipment.

11. Additional Information

1. *Market Research Made Easy*. Don Doman. Dell Dennison and Margaret Doman. Self-Counsel Press, 2002.

2. *Marketing Your Product*. Donald Cyr and Douglas Gray. Self-Counsel Press, 1998

3. *Marketing Your Service*. Jean Withers and Carol Vipperman. Self-Counsel Press, 1998

4. *Advertising Handbook*. Dell Dennison. Self-Counsel Press, 1991.

6. *Winning Proposals*. Hans Tammemagi. Self-Counsel Press, 1999.

7. *Directory of Canadian Trade Commissioner Service*, published by the Canadian Department of Foreign Affairs and International Trade, available at the International Trade Centres.

12
EXPORT SALES CONTRACTS AND DOCUMENTATION

This chapter provides general information about export sales contracts between exporters and foreign buyers and describes the documents required to export goods from Canada. A list of Incoterms, the most commonly used shipping terms, is also included.

1. Export Sales Contracts

Small, one-time orders are usually handled with a purchase order and an invoice. However, large purchases or an agreement for repeat orders are usually handled through some form of export sales contract. The more intricate the business arrangement, the more the necessity for a detailed contract clearly defining the rights and responsibilities of all parties involved. There may also be a law in the target country that requires a contract in order to carry out the transaction.

A sales contract represents the legal relationship between two parties: the buyer and the seller. It serves to clarify the terms of the agreement the two have reached, including the details of the order, product specifications, time frames, transportation, payment terms, and so on. It formalizes in writing contractual terms on which the two parties will base the conduct of their business. The sales contract is enforceable in the legal jurisdiction that governs the contract.

Export contracts are complex and highly specialized. They are governed by a large body of legal precedents, which are increasing in number with the growth of world trade and offshore manufacturing. The requirements and responsibilities are different for every product and service, and for every market. This book can only provide general information on the subject of export sales contracts. Always seek the input of qualified legal counsel in drafting and executing an export sales contract.

2. General Contract Provisions

You should always try to get the contract signed in English and under Canadian law. However, the buyer may insist that the contract be signed in his or her language, particularly if the sale is to a government entity. You may not be able to avoid this necessity, but ensure that the contract is properly translated into English, and preferably reviewed by legal counsel as well, before you execute it.

The contract should be written in plain language, without abbreviations, jargon, or ambiguous terminology. In most cases, it should contain the following basic information and terms.

1. Identification of all parties to the contract.

   Include the buyer, the seller, and/or the seller's agent.

2. Contract date.

   This is important because other dates may be based on this, such as "within 30 days of the contract date Seller will...."

3. Description of the goods and/or services being sold.

   Usually according to the buyer's purchase-order description, but if you normally describe them in another way, include both descriptions in the contract. You may also identify them by the tariff number they will be imported under, depending on the requirements of the customs officials in the importing country.

4. Quantity.

State the number of units or other measure of quantity. Specify the measurement system: imperial if exporting to the United States; and metric to almost every other market in the world. If the measures are approximate, give the range, such as "...within 5 percent of...."

5. Terms and conditions of the goods and services.

Any terms and conditions relating to the specifications, quality of the goods, and so on. If there is a requirement for inspection by a third party, be sure to state who is responsible for the arrangement and payment of the inspection.

6. Terms of the purchase.

What the purchase includes, such as freight, insurance, etcetera. Use the internationally accepted shipping terms based on the INCOTERMS, and write them out in full. See Table 9 for the most common INCOTERMS.

7. Special packing requirements.

Specify the type of packing to be provided and the amount of extra cost for it. This will make a difference to the amount of duty to be paid.

8. Price.

Clearly state the price and the currency. A price breakdown may also be required to calculate the amount of the duty.

9. Method of payment.

Clearly specify the method of payment, related terms, and time frame. If a letter of credit is involved, specify the names of the banks representing each party.

10. Shipping details.

If the purchaser desires a particular shipping method or carrier, this should be stated in the contract. If specific shipping dates are required, these should also be stated.

11. Limitation of responsibilities.

   Allow for your responsibilities to be limited due to specific problems, such as labour disputes at your facilities or transport delays at the docks or airports. You may have to send partial shipments, so you should include a clause allowing for this. Make sure the clause becomes a term in the letter of credit or other payment method.

12. Insurance coverage.

   Ensure that the general terms of the transit insurance are stated, as well as who is responsible for payment. Some purchasers may have a blanket insurance for all of their shipments, and this should also be explained in the contract.

13. Required documentation.

   All documents listed in the purchaser's letter of credit should be listed in the contract. Also state which party is responsible for the preparation of documents.

14. Claims procedures.

   Claims procedures, including time limits, other than loss or damage in shipment, should be included in the contract. Claims relating to transport problems are usually the responsibility of the transport company that shipped the goods, and the purchaser must address the transport company for settlement. This should also be stated in the contract.

3. Documentation

Documentation is a vital part of the exporting process. Without proper documents your purchaser cannot import the goods, and you are unlikely to be paid for them. Commercial goods leaving Canada must be accompanied by several documents. Some of these are required by the federal government under its export regulations, and some are named by the purchaser in the export sales contract and the letter of credit to which you have both agreed.

While the purchaser is generally responsible for telling you what documentation his or her country requires, you can also get this information from freight forwarders and customs brokers. These specialists will investigate the cost of the documents and complete them

TABLE 9
INCOTERMS

The most commonly used shipping terms are standardized in international trade under a set of rules called Incoterms. Incoterms were first published in 1936 by the International Chamber of Commerce, and are periodically updated. Essentially, they establish who assumes what risk and at what cost in the completion of an international sale. Because of the central role they play in export transactions, you should be familiar with them.

1. CIF (cost, insurance, freight) + name of destination:

   This figure includes the basic cost of the goods under discussion, insurance while they are in transit, and transportation charges to the named destination.

2. C&F (cost and freight) or CFR (cost, freight):

   The cost of the goods and freight only. The purchaser is prepared to arrange insurance coverage separately. Some exporters carry insurance over and above that of their purchaser, as a safeguard.

3. C&I (cost and insurance):

   The purchaser will pick up the shipping charges and probably has a blanket agreement with a shipping company to handle the transport of his or her goods.

4. EXW (ex works, ex factory, or ex warehouse):

   This is the cost of the goods at their point of origin, usually your warehouse, and nothing else.

5. FOB (free on board):

   This is the cost of the goods, plus the cost of clearing Canadian customs, and putting them "on board" the chosen transportation mode.

6. FAS (free alongside ship):

   This is the cost of the goods plus the cost of getting them to the point of exit from Canada, including through Canadian customs formalities. The purchaser assumes all other costs.

7. DDP (delivered duty paid or free domicile):

   This includes all of the costs, including import duties, of delivering the goods to the doorstep of the purchaser.

on your behalf as part of their service package. The following sections provide information on the general documentation required.

4. Commercial Documents

4.1 Pro forma invoice

A pro forma invoice is like a quotation or an "invitation to buy," usually in response to a request from the buyer. The document is clearly marked as a "pro forma invoice," and contains the same information as a commercial invoice, becoming a formal order once your buyer accepts and signs it. In countries where foreign funds are limited and foreign payments controlled, the banking authorities sometimes require a pro forma invoice before approving the release of funds to pay for the imported goods. In some circumstances, this can also be used in lieu of a commercial invoice as a customs clearance document.

4.2 Commercial invoice

A commercial invoice is issued by you to your buyer when you have filled the buyer's order and are readying it for shipment. This document confirms the transaction between the two of you and serves as a record of the sale. The commercial invoice clearly identifies your company name, address, and other particulars, and leaves space for the name and particulars of the buyer. It also has space for details of the order placed, including quantity, description, unit price, and extension. The commercial invoice may serve as the customs clearance document in the importer's country, as it does in Canada, and must therefore be complete and accurate. Some countries require that it be accompanied by a sworn statement attesting to its accuracy. The commercial invoice is also the document from which all other documents are prepared.

4.3 Third-party inspection certificate

The buyer may require a third-party inspection certificate as part of the export sales contract. When the buyer is unable to inspect the order before it is shipped, he or she can request that an independent party be retained to inspect it. (Some countries actually require this to be done on all import goods.) Several companies with offices around the world perform this function, supplying you and the buyer with an inspection certificate once they have done their work.

4.4 Packing slip

As the name suggests, a packing slip provides information on how you have packed the buyer's shipment; that is, which products are packed in which box. It is primarily for the convenience of inspectors or customs authorities who wish to examine the goods. It may also detail the size and weight of the boxes, particularly if they are of various dimensions.

4.5 Insurance documents

You may be asked to provide an insurance certificate. It is a preprinted form, available from your insurance company for your completion as the insurer. The insurance certificate is usually made out to your buyer, and contains a description of the goods, their insured value, details of the risks covered, and information on how to make a claim. By endorsing the insurance certificate you transfer the right of claim to the buyer.

4.6 Financial documents

You may be required to provide the buyer with a bill of exchange, depending on the financial arrangements you have made. Two types of bills of exchange are in common use in export/import transactions: a "sight draft" that your buyer pays as soon as it is received; and a "term draft" that is payable after a fixed period specified in the draft.

5. Transportation Documents

5.1 Bill of lading

A bill of lading represents the contract of the carriage between a shipper and a shipping company for the transport of goods to a specific destination. The form itself is supplied by the shipping company, with full contractual details printed on the reverse side, namely the company's responsibilities and liabilities. There are several kinds of bills of lading: truck bills of lading; air bills of lading (air waybill); rail bills of lading; and bills of lading for shipment by sea.

The shipper or his agent supplies all of the information contained in the bill of lading, including the shipper's name, the buyer's name, the name of the party the shipping company must notify once the shipment has arrived (for example, the customs broker), as well as the train, vehicle, or vessel, on which the goods are being shipped.

Space is also provided for a brief description of the goods, their weight and cubic measurement, how they are packed, and whether or not the shipment charges have been paid. Ocean bills of lading include a reference to the number of originals being issued, and the date the shipment is actually stowed on board, with a further stamp that confirms "laden on board."

In the case of ocean bills of lading, once the shipment is in transit, your buyer receives at least two original bills of lading from the shipping company. These are normally airmailed separately on different days in case one goes astray. (This practice dates from the days when the mails were less reliable than they are today.) The buyer usually receives the ocean bills of lading long before the shipment's arrival, and he or she is then contacted again by the shipping company's agent just a few days before the shipment is actually due. To collect the goods, the buyer endorses and presents one of the original bills of lading, which automatically voids all other originals.

5.2 Air waybill

The shipper or his agent receives an air waybill when the shipment is turned over for air transport. The form is numbered, and the first three digits identify the airline being used. This document is not as formal as the ocean bill of lading, and airlines do not issue originals or demand that you present the waybill when you pick up the goods. Instead, they provide copies to you, the carrier, and the purchaser. There is no requirement that the goods be "on board" before a bill is issued, and the date on the bill represents the day when the airline takes possession of the goods, not when they are sent.

6. Official Documents

6.1 Export Declaration (Form B-13)

The export of most goods from Canada is recorded by the government though the completion of a B-13 form, the Export Declaration (see Sample 1). The information collected becomes part of Canada's export trade statistics. The exporter or his agent normally completes the form and submits it to Canada Customs via the shipper at the time and place the goods are exported. The form is not required if—

♦ The shipment is worth less than $500;

SAMPLE 1
CANADA CUSTOMS EXPORT DECLARATION FORM (B-13)

✦ Revenue Revenu Canada Canada	**EXPORT DECLARATION** **DÉCLARATION D'EXPORTATION**	PROTECTED (WHEN COMPLETED) PROTÉGÉ (UNE FOIS REMPLI)	Page of de

1. Canadian Exporter Name and Address - Nom et adresse de l'exportateur canadien	2. Business Number - Numéro d'entreprise	3. Exporter Reference No. N° de référence de l'exportateur

Name - Nom

Street and No. - Rue et n°

City, Country - Ville, pays	Postal Code - Code postal	4. Country of Final Destination Pays de destination finale	5. Customs Assigned Transaction No. N° assigné par les douanes

6. Consignee Name and Complete Address Nom et adresse complète du destinataire	7. Province of Origin - Province d'origine	8. Customs Office of Exit and Date Stamp Timbre dateur du bureau de douane de sortie

Name - Nom

9. Export Permit No. if Applicable
N° du permis d'exportation si applicable

Street and No. - Rue et n°

11(a) Name of Exporting Carrier
Nom du transporteur exportateur

City, Country - Ville, pays

10. Number and Kind of Packages - Nombre et genre de colis	11(b) Vessel Name if Marine Nom du bateau si par eau	12. Currency of Declared Value - Devise de la valeur déclarée

13. Country of Origin ' Pays d'origine	14. Item Description Désignation d'articles	15. HS Commodity Code Code de commodité du SH	16. Qty & Unit of Measure Qté & unité de mesure	17. Value F.O.B Point of Exit Valeur f.à b. bureau de sortie
		18. Gross Weight - Poids brut	19. Total Value F.O.B. Point of Exit Valeur total f.à b. bureau de sortie	

* If foreign goods in same condition as imported, give country of origin.
* S'il s'agit de marchandises étrangères dans l'état ou elles ont été importées indiquer le pays d'origine.

I hereby certify that the information given above and on the continuation sheet(s), if any, is true and complete. Je certifie que les renseignements donnés ci-dessus et sur les feuilles supplémentaires, s'il en est, sont exacts et complets.

24. If Goods are Not Sold, State Reason for Export (If a lease or rental state period)
Si les marchandises ne sont pas vendues, motiver l'exportation (si location ou bail indiquez le terme)

20. Name of Person Responsible for Completion - Nom de la personne responsable de la formule remplie

Street, City - Rue, ville | Province

25. Freight Charges to Point of Exit (Estimated if unknown)
Frais de transport jusqu'au point de sortie (estimatifs si inconnu)

Postal Code - Code postal	Area Code & Tel. No. - Code régional & n° de tél.		Included in Reported Value Inclus dans la valeur	☐ Yes Oui	☐ No Non

$

26. Mode of Transport from Point of Exit
Moyen de transport à partir du lieu de sortie

27. Containerized
Conteneurisées

21. Signature	22. Date	23. Status Statut
		☐ Owner Propr. ☐ Agent

☐ Road Route ☐ Rail Chemin de fer ☐ Water Eau ☐ Air
☐ Other (specify) Autre (précisez)

☐ Yes Oui ☐ No Non

For general information on exports refer to D20-1-1. This directive is published by: ▶ Export Policy, Revenue Canada, Ottawa ON K1A 0L5 (613) 954-7160

For statistical information and export commodity codes contact: ▶ International Trade Division, Statistics Canada, Jean Talon Bldg., Tunney's Pasture, Ottawa ON K1A 0T6 (613) 951-9647 or 1-800-294-5583

For information on controlled exports contact: ▶ Export Controls Division, Dept. of Foreign Affairs and International Trade, Box 481, Station A, Ottawa ON K1N 9K6 (613) 996-2387

Pour les renseignements sur les exportations voir D20-1-1. Cette directive est publiée par : ▶ Politique d'exportation, Revenu Canada, Ottawa ON K1A 0L5 (613) 954-7160

Pour des renseignements statistiques et des codes de commodité d'exportation contacter : ▶ Division du commerce international, Statistique Canada, Imm. Jean Talon, Parc Tunney, Ottawa ON K1A 0T6 (613) 951-9647 ou 1-800-294-5583

Pour des renseignements sur les exportations contrôlées contacter : ▶ Direction du contrôle des exportations, min. des Affaires étrangères et du Commerce international, C.P. 481, Succ. A, Ottawa ON K1N 9K6 (613) 996-2387

B13A (97)

A353

Canada

- The shipment is destined for the United States and is worth less than $2 000 US dollars; and
- The shipment is merely being transported through Canada en route to another foreign destination.

6.2 Certificate of origin

There are two types of certificate of origin. One is required for shipment to the United States or Mexico under the North American Free Trade Agreement (NAFTA); and the second is required by those countries (other than the United States and Mexico) with which Canada has signed a tariff agreement.

The NAFTA certificate of origin (Form B-232E) is perhaps the single most important trade document for shipments within North America. It allows the goods to qualify to enter the United States, Mexico, or Canada under the preferential NAFTA duty rates. Form B-232E must be completed in accordance with the instructions on its reverse side. If it is not completed correctly, the shipper and the buyer may have to pay a fine.

NAFTA requires that the buyer be in possession of a properly completed certificate of origin before he or she can claim the preferential duty rate. A separate certificate should be completed for every qualifying commercial shipment valued at $1 000 US or more. An informal declaration is sufficient for goods of lesser value. For more information on NAFTA, and to view a sample certificate of origin (Sample 2), see Chapter 13, North American Free Trade Agreement.

6.3 Consular invoice

The consular invoice is required by only a few countries, most of them in Latin America. It has two main purposes: to assist the importing country's customs officials in assessing duties and taxes; and to provide trade statistics.

The buyer's embassy or consulate can provide the form. It is usually printed in the official language of the importing country, and requires the same kind of information as a commercial invoice, with a full breakdown of costs. Once the consular invoice is completed you return it to the consulate for "legalization," along with other documents confirming the transaction, such as a commercial invoice. Normally you pay for this service.

6.4 Export permits

Certain products, particularly those related to the military, are under federal government export control. The Canadian Department of Foreign Affairs and International Trade (DFAIT) is responsible for issuing export permits. Please see Chapter 3, Legal Issues, for details and to determine whether these controls affect your product.

6.5 Import licences

The buyer may be required to obtain an import licence from the local government before importing your goods. Always check on this with the buyer or with the appropriate embassy before sending your shipment. Generally the licence number must appear on all documents related to the shipment, and failure to comply with this requirement can result in the goods being held up and you not getting paid. To get an import licence, the buyer may have to present a pro forma invoice to the government authorities several months before the goods are sent.

6.6 Health and other special certificates

Most countries require that health or similar certificates accompany certain imports, such as animals, animal products, plants, and other agricultural products. It is best to check with the embassy of the importing country well ahead of time to determine exactly what is required.

13
NORTH AMERICAN FREE TRADE AGREEMENT

The North American Free Trade Agreement (NAFTA) is a major trade agreement between the United States, Canada, and Mexico. When it was implemented in 1994, it reduced trade barriers among the countries and increased business opportunities. As an exporter, you should know a number of things about NAFTA. This chapter covers most of these points in a broad way and, if you require more detail for your particular business, it refers you to other sources of information.

1. Background

The United States and Canada have a long history of trade agreements between the United States and Canada, most notably in the period since the Second World War, beginning with the Principles of

Economic Cooperation in 1950. The Defense Production Sharing Agreement of 1959 essentially removed the border between the two countries with regard to the development and production of military equipment. The most significant of these bilateral trade agreements was The Auto Pact of 1965, which eliminated tariffs on vehicles and original equipment parts, and in effect, integrated the automotive industry of the two countries. In 1985 these arrangements were reaffirmed in Quebec City by President Reagan and Prime Minister Mulroney.

On January 1, 1989, the United States-Canada Free Trade Agreement (FTA) came into being. This agreement eliminated all tariffs between the United States and Canada on Canadian and American goods. It also reduced or eliminated a number of other trade barriers between the two countries.

The North American Free Trade Agreement, between the United States, Canada, and Mexico, contains many of the provisions of the FTA. It came into effect on January 1, 1994, and in so doing created the world's largest free trade zone. The agreement is still phasing in, but most of its provisions are currently in effect. NAFTA is a very complex agreement, and all its aspects cannot be covered in this book. Additional information pertaining to your export product can be obtained through sources listed in the Additional Information section at the end of this chapter.

The major benefit of NAFTA is the elimination of tariffs among the three countries. Other benefits include:

♦ Allowance of cross-border trade in services such as professional services;

♦ Liberalization of transportation services; and

♦ Better access for professionals such as engineers. (See Appendix A for a list of NAFTA-qualifying professions.)

Two key aspects of NAFTA determine the status of your products with regard to the tariff reduction schedule. The first is the Harmonized Commodity Description and Coding System and the second is the Rules of Origin clause. Both of these are discussed in the next sections.

2. Harmonized Commodity Description and Coding System

The Harmonized Commodity Description and Coding System (HS) is an international, six-digit commodity classification used by American, Canadian, and Mexican customs agencies. The Harmonized System (HS) has several purposes, but the main one is to identify the tariffs that apply to the goods. The Harmonized System is also used for documenting freight and reporting trade statistics among the countries. You can get the HS number for your product by contacting your nearest Canada Customs and Revenue Agency office.

The Harmonized System is very logically structured. Products are arranged into 97 chapters based on economic activity. Each chapter is divided into headings, subheadings, and tariff items. The chapter, heading, and subheading numbers are the same for all the countries using the HS system, and only the last two digits, the tariff items, are assigned by the importing country. For example, all tomato sauces are classified under the HS subheading 2103.20, regardless of the country of import. However, tomato ketchup is specifically classified by tariff item 2103.20.10 in Canada, 2103.20.40 in the United States, and 2103.20.01 in Mexico.

The following example, taken from the Canada Customs and Revenue Agency publication *NAFTA Rules of Origin: Information for Importers, Exporters or Producers*, illustrates this harmonized coding system.

HARMONIZED SYSTEM ITEM 9504.20.21

Chapter 95...........................Toys, games, and sports requisites

Heading 95.04.........................Table or parlour games

Subheading 9504.20....................Articles for billiards and accessories

Tariff item 9504.20.21..................Billiard tables

In order to export to the United States or Mexico under the NAFTA rules, you have to establish the HS number of your product. All associated paperwork will be based on that number.

3. Tariff Reduction Schedules

Before the signing of the Free Trade Agreement between the United States and Canada, more than 70 percent of Canadian exports to the United States were already duty free. The FTA, and then NAFTA, gradually eliminated the remaining tariffs. This elimination was and still is being done in four stages for specific products. The stages are—

- ♦ Immediately at the time the agreement took effect, which was January 1, 1994;
- ♦ Over a five-year period from 1994 to 1998 at the rate of a 20-percent reduction per year;
- ♦ Over a ten-year period from 1994 to 2003 at the rate of a 10-percent reduction per year; and
- ♦ Over a fifteen-year period from 1994 to 2008.

The list of remaining tariffs varies among the countries. For example, the US list of tariffs that are applied to commodities entering the United States from Canada is different from the list of tariffs applied to commodities entering the United States from Mexico. Canada and Mexico have similar but different lists. These lists are gradually reducing in size, and will be totally eliminated by 2008. A list of NAFTA tariff rates by HS number is available at any Canada Customs and Revenue Agency office.

4. Rules of Origin

The origin of a commodity is the most important issue for NAFTA, and the NAFTA certificate of origin is the most important document associated with any cross-border activity. NAFTA, and earlier the FTA, has a clearly defined set of rules to establish the country of origin for each commodity. Goods that are defined as being wholly obtained or produced in the United States and/or Canada qualify for NAFTA tariff rates, as listed in Department of Commerce document STR920300, entitled "Canada—Export Procedures Under the Free Trade Agreement". The definitions, reproduced below, also apply to NAFTA:

1. Mineral goods extracted in the United States, in Canada, or both;
2. Goods harvested in the United States, in Canada, or both;

3. Live animals born and raised in the United States, in Canada, or both;

4. Goods such as fish, shellfish, and other marine life taken from the sea by a vessel that is registered or recorded with Canada or the United States and which flies the flag of Canada or the United States;

5. Goods produced on board a factory vessel from fish, shellfish, and other marine life taken from the sea by a vessel that is registered or recorded with Canada or the United States and which flies the flag of Canada or the United States;

6. Goods taken by Canada, the United States, or a national of either country from or beneath the seabed outside the territorial sea of Canada or the territorial waters of the United States, where Canada or the United States has the right to exploit the seabed or the area beneath the seabed;

7. Goods taken from space where the goods are obtained by Canada, the United States, or a national of either country, and not processed by a third country;

8. Waste and scrap that are derived in the United States or Canada from manufacturing operations and are used goods, where the wastes, scrap, and used goods are collected in the United States or Canada and are fit only for the recovery of raw materials; and

9. Goods produced in the United States or Canada exclusively from goods listed above or from their derivatives, at any stage of production.

The rules also apply to commodities that have portions originating in other countries, prior to being processed in a NAFTA country. For example, teak furniture manufactured in the United States is made with teak wood from another country. The rules of origin allow for the calculation of the portion that is of North American origin, or the Regional Value Content (RVC). There are two ways of calculating the RVC: the transaction value method and the net cost method. Both of these are described in the figure below.

CALCULATION OF REGIONAL VALUE CONTENT

Transaction Value Method

The transaction value method is based on the price at which you sell the item. From this selling price, or transaction value, you subtract the value of non-North American materials and divide the result by the selling price. Here is the method in mathematical form:

$$\frac{\text{(Selling Price)} - \text{(Value of Non-North American Material)}}{\text{Selling Price}} = \text{Percentage of RVC}$$

Net Cost Method

This method is based on the cost of the product. From the total cost of the product you subtract all of your costs (including royalties, shipping, and marketing costs), as well as the value of the non-North American materials. Then you divide the result by the total costs less all of your costs. Here is the method in mathematical form:

$$\frac{\text{(Total Costs)} - \text{(Your Costs} + \text{Cost of Non-North American Materials)}}{\text{(Total Costs)} - \text{(Your Costs)}} = \% \text{ RVC}$$

The certificate of origin is the document that describes the goods being exported. In addition to filling in details such as the names and addresses of the exporter and importer, you also have to provide a description of the goods, the HS tariff classification number, and the country of origin. A sample certificate of origin is shown as Sample 2.

5. Business Travel

NAFTA makes it easier for cross-border movement of business people who are citizens of the member countries. However, it does not change the immigration requirements of the three countries. A good explanation of the NAFTA Cross-Border Movement provisions is given in a pamphlet produced by the Canadian Department of Foreign Affairs and International Trade, entitled "Cross-border Movement and the North American Free Trade Agreement." Much of the information in this section is extracted from the pamphlet. It can be obtained on the Internet at <www.dfait-maeci.gc.ca/nafta-alena /cross-e.asp>. Under NAFTA the four categories of business travellers are as follows:

- ◆ Business visitors;
- ◆ Professionals;

SAMPLE 2
CERTIFICATE OF ORIGIN

Revenue   Revenu
Canada   Canada

PROTECTED (When Completed)

NORTH AMERICAN FREE TRADE AGREEMENT

CERTIFICATE OF ORIGIN

(Instructions Attached)

Please print or type

1 Exporter's Name and Address:		2 Blanket Period:
		From DD MM YY To DD MM YY
	Tax Identification Number: ▶	

3 Producer's Name and Address:		4 Importer's Name and Address:
	Tax Identification Number: ▶	Tax Identification Number: ▶

5 Description of Good(s)	6 HS tariff Classification Number	7 Preference Criterion	8 Producer	9 Net Cost	10 Country of Origin

11 I certify that:

– the information on this document is true and accurate and I assume the responsibility for proving such representations. I understand that I am liable for any false statements or material omissions made on or in connection with this document;

– I agree to maintain, and present upon request, documentation necessary to support this Certificate, and to inform, in writing, all persons to whom the Certificate was given of any changes that would affect the accuracy or validity of this Certificate;

– the goods originated in the territory of one or more of the Parties, and comply with the origin requirements specified for those goods in the North American Free Trade Agreement, and unless specifically exempted in Article 411 or Annex 401, there has been no further production or any other operation outside the territories of the Parties; and

– this Certificate consists of _____ pages, including all attachments.

Authorized Signature:	Company:
Name:	Title:
Date: DD MM YY Telephone:	Fax:

B232 E (98)
Printed in Canada

A430

Canada

- Intra-company transferees; and
- Traders and investors.

Business travellers from any of these four categories may temporarily import certain goods duty-free, if the goods are associated with their activities. Goods allowed include:

- Professional equipment or tools of the trade;
- Equipment for the press, radio, or television broadcasters;
- Cinematographic equipment;
- Sports equipment;
- Goods for display and demonstration;
- Commercial samples;
- Advertising films; and
- Printed advertising materials such as brochures, pamphlets, and catalogues.

6. Business Visitors

Business visitors are business people who plan to carry on any business activity related to research and design; growth; manufacturing and production; marketing; sales and distribution; after-sales service; and general service. You qualify as a business visitor if:

- You are a citizen of a member country;
- You are seeking entry for business purposes;
- The proposed business activity is international in scope;
- You have no intention of entering the labour market;
- Your primary source of remuneration is outside the country in which you are seeking entry;
- The principal place of business, and the accrual of profits, remain outside the country to which you are seeking entry; and
- You meet existing immigration requirements for temporary entry.

Canadian business visitors to the United States or Mexico must meet the general requirements listed above. Generally, no immigration document is issued to a business visitor. However, if terms and conditions are imposed on your entry, you will be issued a visitor record. A visitor record can be useful for frequent cross-border entries or for extended stays. For example, after-sales personnel will be issued a visitor record if the intended stay is to be longer than two days.

After-sales service visits are defined as those —

to install, repair or service, or supervise these functions, or to train workers to perform services, pursuant to a warranty or service contract entered into as an integral part of the sale of commercial or industrial equipment, machinery, or computer software purchased from an enterprise located outside the country where the service is to be provided.

The personnel involved must possess special knowledge essential to the contract requirements.

7. Professionals

Professionals are exempt from the usual process normally required to enter a foreign country's labour market. To qualify as a professional under NAFTA you must meet the following criteria:

- ◆ You are a citizen of a member country;
- ◆ You are to be engaged in an occupation that is listed in NAFTA Appendix 1603.D.1, which includes the educational qualifications associated with the professions (see Appendix A of this book);
- ◆ You are qualified to work in the occupation in which you will be engaged;
- ◆ You have pre-arranged employment or a contractual agreement with an entity located within the country to which you are seeking temporary entry; and
- ◆ You meet existing immigration requirements for temporary entry.

You will have to provide documentation that indicates:

- ◆ The professional level of activity to be carried out;
- ◆ Your job title;
- ◆ A summary of your job duties;
- ◆ Start date and anticipated temporary length of stay; and
- ◆ The arrangement for remuneration.

The documentation can be in the form of:

♦ A signed contract between you and an enterprise; or

♦ A letter from your prospective employer or employers confirming that employment has been offered and accepted; or

♦ A letter from your present employer confirming that you are entering the member country in order to render professional services under a signed contract between your employer and an enterprise located within the country to which entry is being sought. (An enterprise can be an individual.)

In addition to the documentation listed above, you will have to demonstrate your professional qualification, usually with a certified copy of your education credentials. Your proof of citizenship can be shown with your passport. You may also have to prove to the immigration officers that you do not plan to indefinitely reside in the country to which you are seeking entry.

Once you have all the documentation required, you can apply for an employment authorization Citizenship and Immigration Canada (Form IMM1295) at any American or Mexican embassy, consulate, or port-of-entry. There is a processing fee.

8. Intra-Company Transferees

Intra-company transferees are business people employed by an enterprise who are seeking to provide services to a branch, parent, subsidiary, or affiliate of that enterprise, in a managerial or executive capacity, or in a manner that involves specialized knowledge. To qualify as an intra-company transferee you must:

♦ Be a citizen of a member country;

♦ Be seeking employment in an executive or managerial capacity, or one involving specialized knowledge;

♦ Have been engaged in a similar position within the enterprise for at least one year within the previous three years;

♦ Be transferring to an enterprise that has a clear relationship with the enterprise in which you are currently employed; and

♦ Comply with existing immigration requirements for temporary entry.

You can apply for an employment authorization form at any American or Mexican embassy, consulate, or port-of-entry. The employment authorization is initially issued for periods up to one year, but extensions may be granted in increments of up to two years. There is a processing fee. The documentation you require is:

♦ A detailed outline of the purpose and length of stay for which entry is being sought; and

♦ A detailed outline of your current job description, position title, and place in the organizational structure of the enterprise.

9. Traders and Investors

Traders are business people who trade in goods and services between their country of residence and the country to which entry is being sought. To qualify as a trader you must prove that:

♦ You are a citizen of a member country;

♦ The enterprise has the nationality of a member country (at least 50 percent owned by citizens of the country);

♦ Your predominant activity is to carry on substantial trade (exchange, purchase, or sale) in goods or services principally between your present country of residence and the country to which you are seeking entry;

♦ The capacity in which you will be acting is executive or supervisory in nature or involves essential skills; and

♦ You otherwise meet existing immigration requirements for temporary entry.

Investors are business people seeking to establish, develop, administer, or provide advice or key technical services to the operation of an investment to which a substantial amount of capital has been committed or is in the process of being committed. To qualify as an investor you must prove that:

♦ You are a citizen of a member country;

♦ The enterprise has the nationality of a member country (at least 50 percent owned by citizens of the country);

♦ Substantial investment has or is being made;

♦ The investment is more than a marginal one;

- The enterprise is a real and operating commercial enterprise that operates continuously to produce some service or commodity for profit;

- You are in a position to develop and direct the enterprise or, if an employee of an investor, you are in a position that is executive, supervisory, or involves essential skills; and

- You comply with existing immigration requirements for temporary entry.

As a trader or investor you can apply for an employment authorization form at any American or Mexican embassy or consulate. There is a processing fee. You will also be required to provide information on your business by completing an Application for Trader/Investor Status.

10. Settling Trade Disputes

NAFTA has a carefully defined dispute settlement process. Under NAFTA, a Free Trade Commission is set up that has a senior trade representative, or designated alternate, from each member country. Supporting the Commission is a permanent Secretariat with offices in each country. The Secretariat attempts to avoid disputes, or solve them through consultation. When this fails, the issue is raised to the level of the Commission itself.

The Commission members can call for an arbitration panel to be set up to resolve the dispute. The panels are made up of five members chosen from a list of professionals approved by all member countries. The panel can call on experts to assist them in their decision. The procedures are conducted under strict deadlines to ensure that disputes are settled as quickly as possible.

11. Doing Business in the United States

The United States is by far Canada's largest export market. Although our language is the same and our cultures are somewhat similar, there are subtle differences in the way Americans do business.

Doing business in the United States requires a good grasp of both American business practices and the structure of the American market. Among the Canadian products already exported to the United States, those with unusual or distinctive characteristics have been the most successful. It is very difficult to enter the American market with a "me too" product that is already being supplied by US companies. If yours is such a product, try to give it a unique spin to distinguish it from the local variety.

One of the more common errors beginning exporters make when approaching the American market is to base the market potential for their products on American gross market figures. In fact, the United States has the most segmented market of any nation in the world. Their gross figures tell you little about where and how to make your entry. It is better to identify how your product might be used, and the potential customers most likely to use it. Then determine where most of these customers live, and target that part of the United States.

The initial information gathering about the US market is made easier by the fact that the United States is among the most studied markets in the world. Information is widely available from both the American and Canadian governments, as well as trade associations and marketing firms that specialize in pre-packaged market studies. You will also find that industry contacts are usually prepared to talk to you by telephone, as long as you are well-informed about the industry and can provide them with information in exchange.

The Canadian government has consulates in major cities throughout the United States. Contact the trade officials in the city nearest your target market and get as much information as you can from them. Trade officials conduct numerous studies on the markets in their areas and publish them for the use of Canadian business people. Chances are they may even have studied your specific product area. You will be pleasantly surprised at how useful these officials can be. In addition to the Canadian embassy in Washington, DC, Canadian consulates are located in the following American cities:

- ◆ Atlanta;
- ◆ Boston;
- ◆ Buffalo;
- ◆ Chicago;
- ◆ Dallas;
- ◆ Detroit;
- ◆ Los Angeles;
- ◆ Miami;

- ♦ Minneapolis;
- ♦ New York;
- ♦ San Francisco/Silicon Valley; and
- ♦ Seattle.

Once you know your target market, have a look at how its buyers prefer to make their purchases, and consider using the same approach. Do they deal directly with the manufacturer, or with an agent or distributor? Many American buyers prefer to buy from a local agent, so you may want to review Chapter 10, Retaining an Agent.

Always quote your prices in US dollars, and include shipping costs and brokerage fees. It is important to be viewed as a domestic supplier by your customers, with the same ability to respond to orders as your American competitor. The last thing these customers want to address is the issue of importing the product across the border. In this regard, having an American address can help your sales. It can be as simple as a post office box in a border town, or a commercial office from which all mail and telephone calls are forwarded to your Canadian facilities.

12. Doing Business in Mexico

Mexican business practices are an extension of the social traditions of Mexican society. Family is central to the Mexican way of life, and business organizations tend to be established along traditional hierarchical lines with a single, respected decision-maker in charge. So decisions rest with only the most senior staff, and even highly qualified employees are unwilling to comment on their senior's actions. Honour holds an important place in the culture's personal value system, and special care should be taken to avoid embarrassing anyone. Mexicans are very reluctant to say "No," and will go to extremes to avoid doing so.

Personal relationships are highly valued in Mexico, and it is important to maintain a warm rapport with business associates. Mexicans also prefer to do business face to face rather than on the telephone. In general, people are formal and business is conducted in a formal, socially sanctioned manner. So business in Mexico takes time to develop.

Bribery, called "la mordida" (the bite), is not as prevalent as it was, but it can still be a cost of doing business in Mexico. You may encounter bribery in the public sector, when you apply for licences and permits, and in the private sector as well. In recent years, the government and local businesses have tried to stamp it out, but it still exists. The best thing for you to do is to let your agent handle any of these situations for you.

Since NAFTA was signed there has been a proliferation of companies that facilitate business between Canada and Mexico. These companies can be useful, but be as cautious as you would be when finding a potential agent. Probably your best initial approach is to contact the Canadian embassy in Mexico to obtain a list of potential agents. The embassy can also provide you with numerous publications relevant to the Mexican market. You can find out more about available services from their Web site at <www.canada.org.mx/english/index.htm>. The Canadian embassy can be reached through your nearest International Trade Centre, or directly at:

Canadian Embassy
Calle Schiller No. 529
Colonia Rincon Del Bosque
11560 Polanco, Mexico, D.F, Mexico
Apartado Postal 105-05
11560 Mexico, D.F., Mexico
Telephone: 011-525-724-7900
Fax: 011-525-724-7982

13. Additional Information

The Internet has a wealth of information about NAFTA. The following Web sites are well worth exploring and bookmarking for future use. Additional resources are available in print.

1. *NAFTA* "Rules of Origin," published by Revenue Canada.

2. "Cross-Border Movement and the North American Free Trade Agreement," published by the Canadian Department of Foreign Affairs and International Trade. Available on the Internet at <www.infoexport.gc.ca/NAFTA/cross-border/16006-e.asp>.

3. *The North American Free Trade Agreement (NAFTA)*, published by the Canadian Department of foreign Affairs and International Trade, available on the Internet at <www.dfait-maeci.gc.ca/NAFTA-alena/menu-e.asp>.

4. "Canada-Export Procedures Under the Free Trade Agreement," US Department of Commerce document STR920300.

5. Industry Canada STRATEGIS Internet site, <strategis.ic.gc.ca>.

6. Canadian embassy in Mexico Web site at <www.canada.org.mx/english/index.htm>.

14
EXPORTING
PROBLEMS

You can face potential problems with exporting, as you can with any other aspect of your business. This chapter touches on some of the more common problems.

1. Agent Issues

Agent issues are the most prevalent exporting problem, because agents are your key contacts in the foreign market. The first problem you may encounter with an agent is a lot of pressure from him to sign an agreement. Some of the more unscrupulous agents will even refuse to talk to you unless you sign an agreement with them. You don't have to work with people like that. There are plenty of legitimate agents who would like your business. A good agent will often suggest that you not make a formal agreement until he tests the market with your product. Then when he knows he can sell it, he will make a deal with you. The agent may want a letter of intent from you that states you will do business with him if he finds customers for you, and it is quite safe for you to give him one. Do not be pressured into signing an agent agreement until you are sure you want to do business with a particular agent.

The next problem you may run into with an agent is a lack of activity on your behalf. This is quite common. Before you jump on an apparently inactive agent, make sure you have been giving him the support he needs, not only a steady supply of brochures, but also a good knowledge of the product, particularly if it is fairly technical. If he has the support he needs, you might then begin by asking him if he is having trouble selling your product. Ask him what you can do to help. If this question doesn't get your agent moving, be a bit more forceful. When all else fails and your agent is still not producing any business for you, cancel the agreement and find somebody else.

You can also have the opposite problem — an overactive agent — one that wants you to respond to every inquiry he gets about your product, rather than qualifying it himself before he asks you to make a quote or proposal. You can spend a lot of time dealing with this kind of agent, with little to show for it. You can try to get your agent to do more qualification by asking him questions about the customer before you respond. Once he gets the answers to these questions he may realize that he overreacted. Hopefully after a few of these incidents, your agent will learn to contact you only with real business opportunities.

2. Competing Agents

Just as your agent maintains the presence of your company in a foreign country, so too do other agents represent your competitors. They will do what they can to influence the customer in their favour, and often against you. You can sometimes see this competition openly when you are briefing a group of potential customers, and one member of the audience asks very knowledgeable and embarrassing questions. He is either from a competing agency or that agent has briefed him on the shortcomings of your product. His goal is to get his colleagues to decline your product and select the one that he is representing.

In some countries, and for some products, your competitors will pay agents just to keep the customer from buying your product. These agents can use anything from the simple tactic of planting a competitor in the audience described in the previous paragraph, to a sophisticated disinformation campaign. Disinformation campaigns are usually associated with big projects for which your competitor is trying to buy time until his product has been developed. They are not uncommon in the military business. There is little you can do about them other than to ensure that your agent is able to fend off the attacks.

3. Government Corruption

Government corruption is common throughout the world. The usual form is the bribery needed to speed up the issuance of permits. However, there are also many countries in which government officials demand kickbacks or payoffs for doing business with you. Russia, for example, is rife with both of these problems. In most cases you will not know it is going on, because your agent is handling these problems. Often they are the reason agent fees in countries with corrupt governments are higher than other places.

There is not much you can do about corruption, short of giving up the business. Payoffs have been going on for centuries and, despite international efforts to stop corruption, it will probably continue. There are just too many international business people, mainly from some European and Asian countries, who rely on corruption to sell inferior products.

4. Sucker Bids

Sucker bids are a particularly dirty trick that is pulled on the novice exporter. They usually take place with government purchasing, but can also happen if you are dealing with a large industrial company. The situation arises when the buyer must prove that he or she looked at several suppliers before choosing the one that has offered him personal benefits. He or she gets the proof he needs by asking other companies to bid on the project, even though he or she has no intention of doing business with them. You can thus end up spending a lot of effort and money just to help somebody else get the business.

A good agent should be attuned to the problem of sucker bids and not get suckered in himself. If you suspect there is a problem, try to get more information about the opportunity through your agent. Find out who the other bidders are and what their relationships are to the buyer. Canadian embassy trade officials may also be able to help you. However, in the end it will probably be left up to your judgement to decide whether or not you should expend resources on pursuing the opportunity.

5. Industrial Espionage

Industrial espionage is real, and Canadian companies are being targeted. If you have a high-tech product, you could be under attack and not even know it. You are particularly vulnerable during international marketing activities. A typical approach is for the competitor to buy your product and reverse engineer it. You can't do much to stop this except design the product to minimize the information that would be obtained from reverse engineering, but that isn't easy to do.

Trade shows are a great opportunity for industrial espionage. In one incident competitors broke into a booth at night, disassembled a product on display, and photographed the insides. Although this example is somewhat amateurish, the pros are at it as well. A few years ago, the US government warned American companies that the French spy agency had been tasked to get information on US technology at the Paris Air Show. Can you imagine what is going on at trade shows in places such as Dubai, Malaysia, or Shanghai?

6. Customer Issues

Customer issues are usually associated with late delivery, incomplete delivery, and customs clearance. Your agent usually deals with minor customer problems, at least initially. Try to have your agent solve as many of the problems as possible, because often the source of the problem is in the foreign country. With both of you working to solve the problem, you will both learn from the incident and hopefully prevent it from happening again.

One of the more difficult customer issues is a lack of understanding of the technology involved in the product. Just think of the trouble you and your family have programming your VCR. Now extend that analogy to a customer who is unfamiliar with technology in general, who is operating in a different language, and who has a limited education. For example, a commercial fisherman who has just bought an expensive fish-finding sonar, but knows little about it, has slim chances of setting it correctly for his waters and having it work as advertised. Naturally, the fisherman will complain to the agent, and in turn to you. The fix is to train the customer how to work the equipment.

Helping your customers understand your technology can be a daunting and expensive task. You may be able to solve some problems over the telephone, and an 800 number can help your North American customers. But, for the rest of the world, you will have to put a lot of faith in your agent. You will have to train your agent so he can train your customers and answer their questions. Once again, your selection of an agent is very important.

15
SHIPPING YOUR SALES

If your product involves goods or equipment associated with a service, you will have to ship your sales to the foreign buyer. This chapter describes the services available to help you in this regard, and details the documentation you will require.

1. Freight Forwarders and Brokers

Freight forwarders are one of a general group of transport specialists, called freight intermediaries, who facilitate the shipment of goods from the seller to the buyer. Also included in this title are transportation brokers. Both forwarders and brokers can act as the principal or agent in a freight transaction. As the principal, the intermediary assumes responsibility (and liability) for every aspect of the shipment until it is delivered to the buyer. As agent, the intermediary is responsible only until the shipment has been delivered into the carrier's possession.

Brokers find the best carrier at the best price for the seller's needs. Forwarders consolidate small shipments into a single large shipment for transport and, once the freight reaches the destination terminal, the forwarders break out the small shipments and arrange for delivery. In this capacity the forwarder acts as principal, and is usually named as the principal or shipper on any commercial documents provided by the carrier.

Part of the freight forwarder's job is to ensure that all documentation pertaining to the shipment is completed and in order. The forwarder can advise and assist the shipper in documentation preparation, select the fastest and most cost-effective route for the shipment, and even take payment for it on behalf of the shipper. By employing a freight forwarder, a shipper is relieved of negotiating with individual carriers at each step in the shipment process. International forwarders are of two types: ocean freight forwarders and air freight forwarders.

1.1 Ocean freight forwarders

Ocean freight forwarders are also referred to as "non-vessel owning" (NVO) carriers, or "non-vessel operating common carriers" (NVOCC) in the United States. They consolidate small shipments into single-container shipments destined for the same foreign port.

1.2 Air freight forwarders

Air freight forwarders must belong to the International Air Transport Association IATA before they can act as official agents for airlines. They can represent shippers as either principal or agent, however. As principal for shippers, they consolidate small shipments into unit loading devices (ULDS) destined for the same foreign airport and take full responsibility for the shipments. As agent for airlines, they arrange shipments through the carriers they represent and receive a commission from the carrier for this work. The carriers in this case are liable for the shipments.

Canadian freight forwarders have their own professional organization, the Canadian International Freight Forwarders Association (CIFFA). You can learn more about the CIFFA and get a list of their members at their Web site <www.ciffa.com>, or by contacting their head office at:

Canadian International Freight Forwarders Association
1243 Islington Avenue, Suite 706
Etobicoke, ON M8X 1Y9
Telephone: (416) 234-5100
Fax: (416) 234-5152

2. Customs Brokers

Customs brokers are commercial companies that help importers get through the complex process of bringing goods into a country. They are usually licensed by the government to carry out customs-related responsibilities on behalf of their clients. Customs brokers charge a fee for their services, which include:

♦ Advising you on tariff classifications, duty rates, fees, rules of origin, and other pertinent issues;

♦ Obtaining, preparing, and presenting or transmitting the necessary documents or data;

♦ Paying, on your behalf, any duties that apply;

♦ Obtaining release of the imported goods;

♦ Maintaining records; and

♦ Responding to any customs-related concerns after payment.

It is highly recommended that you use a customs broker, at least for your initial shipments into a country. The documentation and bureaucracy are far too complex for you to deal with comfortably. Probably the easiest way for you to get a customs broker is to have your agent recommend one. Your freight forwarder should also be able to help you find one.

3. Documentation Required

The documentation required to ship your exports into a country are usually of three different categories. These are listed below, and are further explained in Chapter 12, Export Sales Contracts and Documentation.

3.1 Commercial documents

Commercial documents are associated with the purchase and payment itself, and can include any of the following:

◆ Pro forma invoice;

◆ Commercial invoice;

◆ Third-party inspection certificate;

◆ Packing list;

◆ Insurance documents; and

◆ Financial documents.

3.2 Transportation documents

Transportation documents relate to the shipping activity itself and, depending on the mode of transportation, can be either:

◆ Bill of lading; or

◆ Air way bill.

3.3 Official documents

Official documents are required by the Canadian government and the government of the importing country. They can include any of the following:

◆ Export declaration (B-13);

◆ Certificate of origin;

◆ Consular invoice;

◆ Export permit;

◆ Import licence; and

◆ Health and other special certificates.

4. Special NAFTA Requirements and Documentation

There are special requirements and documentation under the North American Free Trade Agreement when you are exporting to the United States and Mexico. These are discussed in Chapter 13, the North American Free Trade Agreement. You can also get considerable information from the publication "Cross-Border Movement and the North American Free Trade Agreement," published by the Canadian Department of Foreign Affairs and International Trade, and available on the Internet at <www.infoexport.gc.ca/nafta/cross-border/16006-e.asp>.

The main document you will have to deal with is the certificate of origin, a sample of which is shown in Chapter 13. The main information required on this form includes:

- ◆ Name and address of exporter;
- ◆ Name and address of importer;
- ◆ Description of the goods;
- ◆ HS tariff classification number;
- ◆ Country of origin; and
- ◆ Regional value content (Canadian content).

5. Additional Information

The Internet has a wealth of information about shipping your export sales. The following Web sites are well worth exploring and bookmarking for future use.

1. Canadian International Freight Forwarders Association (CIFFA) Web site <www.ciffa.com>.

2. "Cross-Border Movement and the North American Free Trade Agreement," published by the Canadian Department of Foreign Affairs and International Trade, and available on the Internet at <www.infoexport.gc.ca/nafta/cross-border/16006-e.asp>.

Appendix A
NAFTA-QUALIFYING PROFESSIONS

This appendix provides a list of professions recognized under the North American Free Trade Agreement. It is extracted from the NAFTA Appendix 1603.D.1: Professionals.

Profession	Minimum Education Requirements and Alternative Credentials
General	
Accountant	Baccalaureate or licenciatura degree; or C.P.A., C.G.A. or C.M.A.
Architect	Baccalaureate or licenciatura degree; or state/provincial licence
Computer Systems Analyst	Baccalaureate or licenciatura degree; or post-secondary diploma or post-secondary Certificate 4, and three years' experience
Disaster Relief Insurance Claims Adjuster	Baccalaureate or licenciatura degree, and successful completion of training in the appropriate areas of insurance adjustment

Economist	Baccalaureate or licenciatura degree
Engineer	Baccalaureate or licenciatura degree; or state/provincial licence
Forester	Baccalaureate or licenciatura degree; or state/provincial licence
Graphic Designer	Baccalaureate or licenciatura degree; or post-secondary diploma or post-secondary Certificate, and three years' experience
Hotel Manager	Baccalaureate or licenciatura degree in hotel/restaurant management; or post-secondary diploma or post-secondary certificate in hotel/restaurant management, and three years' experience in hotel/restaurant management
Industrial Designer	Baccalaureate or licenciatura degree; or post-secondary diploma or post-secondary certificate, and three years' experience
Interior Designer	Baccalaureate or licenciatura degree; or post-secondary diploma or post-secondary certificate, and three years' experience
Land Surveyor	Baccalaureate or licenciatura degree; or state/provincial/ federal licence
Landscape Architect	Baccalaureate or licenciatura degree
Lawyer (including Notary)	LL.B., J.D., LL.L., B.C.L. or licenciatura degree (five years); or membership in a state/provincial bar
Librarian	M.L.S. or B.L.S. (for which another baccalaureate or licenciatura degree was a prerequisite)
Management Consultant	Baccalaureate or licenciatura degree; or equivalent professional experience as established by statement or professional credential attesting to five years' experience as a management consultant, or five years' experience in a field of specialty related to the consulting agreement
Mathematician (including Statistician)	Baccalaureate or licenciatura degree
Range Manager/Range Conservationalist	Baccalaureate or licenciatura degree
Research Assistant (working in a post-secondary educational institution)	Baccalaureate or licenciatura degree
Scientific Technician/ Technologist	Possession of (a) theoretical knowledge of any of the following disciplines: agricultural sciences, astronomy, biology, chemistry, engineering, forestry, geology, geophysics, meteorology or physics; and (b) the ability to solve practical problems in any of those disciplines, or the ability to apply principles of any of those disciplines to basic or applied research

Social Worker	Baccalaureate or licenciatura degree
Sylviculturist (including Forestry Specialist)	Baccalaureate or licenciatura degree
Technical Publications Writer	Baccalaureate or licenciatura degree; or post-secondary diploma or post-secondary certificate, and three years' experience
Urban Planner (including Geographer)	Baccalaureate or licenciatura degree
Vocational Counsellor	Baccalaureate or licenciatura degree

Medical/Allied Professional

Dentist	D.D.S., D.M.D., Doctor en Odontologia or Doctor en Cirugia Dental; or state/provincial licence
Dietitian	Baccalaureate or licenciatura degree; or state/provincial licence
Medical Laboratory Technologist	Baccalaureate or licenciatura degree; or post-secondary diploma or post-secondary certificate, and three years' experience
Nutritionist	Baccalaureate or licenciatura degree
Occupational Therapist	Baccalaureate or licenciatura degree; or state/provincial licence
Pharmacist	Baccalaureate or licenciatura degree; or state/provincial licence
Physician (teaching or research only)	M.D. or Doctor en Medicina; or state/provincial licence
Physiotherapist/Physical Therapist	Baccalaureate or licenciatura degree; or state/provincial licence
Psychologist	State/provincial licence; or licenciatura degree
Recreational Therapist	Baccalaureate or licenciatura degree
Registered Nurse	State/provincial licence; or licenciatura degree
Veterinarian	D.V.M., D.M.V. or Doctor en Veterinaria; or state/provincial licence

Scientist

Agriculturist (including Agronomist)	Baccalaureate or licenciatura degree
Animal Breeder	Baccalaureate or licenciatura degree
Animal Scientist	Baccalaureate or licenciatura degree
Apiculturist	Baccalaureate or licenciatura degree
Astronomer	Baccalaureate or licenciatura degree

Biochemist	Baccalaureate or licenciatura degree
Biologist	Baccalaureate or licenciatura degree
Chemist	Baccalaureate or licenciatura degree
Dairy Scientist	Baccalaureate or licenciatura degree
Entomologist	Baccalaureate or licenciatura degree
Epidemiologist	Baccalaureate or licenciatura degree
Geneticist	Baccalaureate or licenciatura degree
Geologist	Baccalaureate or licenciatura degree
Geochemist	Baccalaureate or licenciatura degree
Geophysicist (including Oceanographer in Mexico and the United States)	Baccalaureate or licenciatura degree
Horticulturist	Baccalaureate or licenciatura degree
Meteorologist	Baccalaureate or licenciatura degree
Pharmacologist	Baccalaureate or licenciatura degree
Physicist (including Oceanographer in Canada)	Baccalaureate or licenciatura degree
Plant Breeder	Baccalaureate or licenciatura degree
Poultry Scientist	Baccalaureate or licenciatura degree
Soil Scientist	Baccalaureate or licenciatura degree
Zoologist	Baccalaureate or licenciatura degree

Teacher

College	Baccalaureate or licenciatura degree
Seminary	Baccalaureate or licenciatura degree
University	Baccalaureate or licenciatura degree

Appendix B
Federal Government
Export Assistance Offices

The following is a listing of Canadian federal government offices that can help the Canadian exporter. It is taken directly from a part of the infoexport Web site at <www.infoexport.gc.ca/PEMD_annex-e.asp>, which you may want to visit for updates. The listing is divided into four areas, the main one being a listing of the International Trade Centres across Canada.

1. International Trade Centres

BRITISH COLUMBIA
(includes responsibility for Yukon)
300 West Georgia St., Suite 2000
Vancouver, British Columbia V6B 6E1
Tel: (604) 666-1443/Fax: (604) 666-0954

ALBERTA
(includes responsibility for Northwest Territories)
Canada Place, 9700 Jasper Ave., Suite 725
Edmonton, Alberta T5J 4C3
Tel: (780) 495-2944/Fax: (780) 495-4507

639–5th Avenue S.W., Suite 400
Calgary, Alberta T2P 0M9
Tel: (403) 292-4575/Fax: (403) 292-4578

SASKATCHEWAN
Princeton Tower, 7th Floor
123-2nd Avenue South
Saskatoon, Saskatchewan S7K 7E6
Tel: (306) 975-5315/Fax: (306) 975-5334

1919 Saskatchewan Drive, 2nd Floor
Regina, Saskatchewan S4P 3N8
Tel: (306) 780-6124/Fax: (306) 780-8797

MANITOBA
(Mail: P.O. Box 981, R3C 2V2)
400 St. Mary Avenue, 4th Floor
Winnipeg, Manitoba R3C 4K5
Tel: (204) 983-4540/Fax: (204) 983-3182

ONTARIO
151 Yonge Street, 4th Floor
Toronto, Ontario M5J 2W7
Tel: (416) 973-5053/Fax: (416) 973-8161

QUEBEC
5 Place Ville-Marie, 7th Floor, Suite 800
Montreal, Quebec, H3B 2G2
Tel: (514) 283-6328/Fax: (514) 283-8794

OR

Canada Economic Development for Quebec Regions

Abitibi-Témiscamingue Region
906–5th Avenue
Val d'Or, Quebec J9P 1B9
Tel: (819) 825-5260/Fax: (819) 825-3245

Bas-Saint-Laurent/Gaspésie/Îles-de-la Madeleine Region
2 St. Germain St. East, Suite 310
Rimouski, Quebec G5L 8T7
Tel: (418) 722-3282/Fax: (418) 722-3285

North Shore Region
701 Laure Boulevard, P.O. Box 698, Suite 202B
Sept-Iles, Quebec G4R 4K9
Tel: (418) 968-3426/Fax: (418) 968-0806

Estrie Region
65 Belvedere St. North, Suite 240
Sherbrooke, Quebec J1H 4A7
Tel: (819) 564-5905/Fax: (819) 564-5912

Laval/Laurentides/Lanaudière Region
Triomphe II Tower
2540 Daniel-Johnson Blvd., Suite 204
Laval, Quebec H7T 2S3
Tel: (450) 973-6844/Fax: (450) 973-6851

Centre du Québec
Place du Centre
150 Marchand St., Suite 502
Drummondville, Quebec J2C 4N1
Tel: (819) 478-4664/Fax: (819) 478-4666

Mauricie Region
Le Bourg du Fleuve
25 des Forges St., 4th Floor, Suite 413
Trois-Rivières, Quebec G9A 2G4
Tel: (819) 371-5182/Fax: (819) 371-5186

Montérégie Region
1111 St-Charles St. West, Suite 411
Longueuil, Quebec J4K 5G4
Tel: (450) 928-4088/Fax: (450) 928-4097

Montréal Region
800 Square Victoria, Suite 3800, P.O. Box 247
Montreal, Quebec H4Z 1E8
Tel: (514) 283-2500/Fax: (514) 496-8310

Outaouais Region
259 St-Joseph Blvd., 2nd Floor, Suite 202
Hull, Quebec J8Y 6T1
Tel: (819) 994-7442/Fax: (819) 994-7846

Québec/Chaudière-Appalaches Region
112 Dalhousie St., 2nd Floor
Quebec, Quebec G1K 4C1
Tel: (418) 648-4826/Fax: (418) 648-7291

Saguenay/Lac-Saint-Jean Region
170 St-Joseph St. South, Suite 203
Alma, Quebec G8B 3E8
Tel: (418) 668-3084/Fax: (418) 668-7584

NEW BRUNSWICK
1045 Main St., Unit 103
Moncton, New Brunswick E1C 1H1
Tel: (506) 851-6452/Fax: (506) 851-6429

NOVA SCOTIA
1800 Argyle Street, Fifth Floor
World Trade & Convention Centre
(Mail: P.O. Box 940, Station M)
Halifax, Nova Scotia B3J 2V9
Tel: (902) 426-7540/Fax: (902) 426-5218

PRINCE EDWARD ISLAND
75 Fitzroy Street
P.O. Box 1115, Charlottetown, PEI C1A 7M8
Tel: (902) 566-7426/Fax: (902) 566-7377

NEWFOUNDLAND
John Cabot Building, 10th Floor
Phase II, 10 Barter's Hill
P.O. Box 8950
St. John's, Newfoundland A1B 3R9
Tel: (709) 772-5511/Fax: (709) 772-5093

NORTHWEST TERRITORIES
See Alberta

YUKON
See British Columbia

2. Infocentre

For program application forms, or for general trade inquiries, please call:

Toll-free: 1-800-267-8376
Ottawa area: (613) 944-4000
Fax: (613) 996-9709
FaxLink: (613) 944-4500
E-mail: enqserv@dfait-maeci.gc.ca
Internet: www.dfait-maeci.gc.ca

3. Win Exports

For information on WIN Exports, visit DFAIT's Website at <www.dfait-maeci.gc.ca>.

To register in WIN Exports, please contact: 1-800-551-4946 or (613) 944-4946 in Ottawa, or fax your request to 1-800-667-3802 or (613) 944-1078.

4. Export Programs/Export Information

For information on other export market development programs, visit the following Web sites:

Program for Export Market Development – Investment (PEMD-I):
www.dfait-maeci.gc.ca/investcan

PEMD Agri-Food: www.agr.ca

For General Export Information:

www.infoexport.gc.ca
www.cbsc.org
Team Canada: Toll free: 1-888-811-1119
24-hour fax line: 1-888-449-5444

Appendix C
PROVINCIAL GOVERNMENT
EXPORT ASSISTANCE OFFICES

The following is a list of provincial government offices that offer various forms of export assistance to companies located in their province.

Alberta
Alberta Economic Development Authority
McDougall Centre
455 – 6th Street S.W.
Calgary, AB T2P 4E8
Tel: (403) 297-3022
Fax: (403) 297-6435
Government Web site is

British Columbia

International Services Branch
Ministry of Employment and Investment
999 Canada Place, Suite 730
Vancouver, BC V6C 3E1
Telephone: (604) 844-1837
Government directory Web site at

Manitoba

Manitoba Trade and Investment Corporation
410–155 Carlton Street
Winnipeg, MB R3C 3H8
Telephone: (204) 945-2466 or toll free at 1-800-529-9981
Government Web site is <www.gov.mb.ca/itt/trade/index.html>

New Brunswick

Visit the New Brunswick Business Service Centre at:
Trade Branch
Economic Development Tourism and Culture
670 King Street, Room 549
PO Box 6000
Fredericton, NB E3B 5H1
Telephone: (506) 453-3649 or toll free at 1-800-668-1010
Government Web site <www.gov.nb.ca/edt/econdev.asp>

Newfoundland and Labrador

Department of Industry Trade and Technology
Government of Newfoundland and Labrador
PO Box 8700
St. John's, NF A1B 4J6
Telephone: (709) 729-5600 or (709) 729-5936
Government Web site at

Nova Scotia

Investment and Trade Directorate
Telephone: (902) 424-5659
Fax: (902) 424-5739
Government Web site at

Ontario

Trade Development Division/Ontario Exports Inc.
Sunco, 7th Floor
56 Wellesley Street West
Toronto, ON M7A 2E4
Telephone: (416) 314-8200 or toll free at 1-877-468-7233
Web site <www.ontario-canada.com/export>

Prince Edward Island

Prince Edward Island Business Development Inc.
Trade and Export Development
Third and Fourth Floors, Holman Building
25 University Avenue
PO Box 910
Charlottetown, PE C1A 7L9
Government Web site at <www.gov.pe.ca/development/index.php3>

Quebec

Ministry of Industry and Commerce
710, Place d'Youville
Quebec, PQ G1R 4Y4
Telephone: (418) 691-5950
Fax: (418) 644-0118
Government Web site at

Ministry of Industry and Commerce
380, rue St. Antoine Ouest
Montreal, PQ H27 3X7
Telephone: (514) 499-2550
Fax: (514) 873-9913

Saskatchewan

Saskatchewan Economic and Co-operative Development
1919 Saskatchewan Drive
Regina, SK S4P 3V7
Telephone: (306) 787-2232
Fax: (306) 787-2159
Government Web site <www.gov.sk.ca/govt/econdev/>

Saskatchewan Economic and Co-operative Development
206–15 Innovation Boulevard
Saskatoon, SK S7N 2X8
Telephone: (306) 933-7200
Fax: (306) 933-8244

Appendix D
TRADE AND INDUSTRY ORGANIZATIONS

The following is a list of organizations that offer various forms of export assistance to their member companies.

Aerospace Industries Association of Canada
60 Queen Street, Suite 1200
Ottawa, ON K1P 5Y7
Telephone: (613) 232-4297
Fax: (613) 232-1142
Web site: www.aiac.ca

Alliance of Manufacturers and Exporters Canada
75 International Boulevard, Suite 400
Toronto, ON M9W 6L9
Telephone: (416) 798-8000
Fax: (416) 798-8050

Automotive Industries Association of Canada
1272 Wellington Street
Ottawa, ON K1Y 3A7
Telephone: (613) 728-5821
Fax: (613) 728-6021
E-mail: aia@aiacanada.com
Web site: http://www.aftmkt.com/associations/AIA

Automotive Parts Manufacturers Association
195 The West Mall, Suite 516
Toronto, ON M9C 5K1
Telephone: (416) 620-4220
Fax: (416) 620-9730
E-mail: apma@interware.net

Canadian Association of Mining Equipment and Services for Export
345 Renfrew Drive, Suite 101
Markham, ON L3R 9S9
Telephone: 1-905-513-0046
Fax: 1-905-513-1834
E-mail: MINESUPPLY@CAMESE.ORG

Canadian Association of Petroleum Producers
350–7 Avenue SW, Suite 2100
Calgary, AB T2P 3N9
Telephone: (403) 267-1100
Fax: (403) 261-4122
E-mail: communication@capp.ca

Canadian Chemical Producers' Association
Toll free: 1-800-267-6666
Fax: (613) 237-4061

Canadian Concrete Pipe Association
979 Derry Road East
Mississauga, ON L5T 2J7
Toll free: 1-800-435-0116
Telephone: (905) 565-0380
Fax: (905) 565-0346
E-mail: ccpa@ican.ca

Canadian Construction Association
75 Albert Street, Suite 400
Ottawa, ON K1P 5E7
Telephone: (613) 236-9455
Fax: (613) 236-9526

Canadian Drilling Association
306–222 McIntyre Street West
North Bay, ON P1B 2Y8
Telephone: (705) 476-6992
Fax: (705) 476-9494
E-mail: mineval@vianet.on.ca

Canadian Paint and Coatings Association
9900 Cavendish Boulevard, Suite 103
St-Laurent, PQ H4M 2V2
Telephone: (514) 745-2611
Fax: (514) 745-2031
E-mail: cpca@cam.org

Canadian Plastics Industry Association
5925 Airport Road, Suite 500
Mississauga, ON L4V 1W1
Telephone: (905) 678-7748
Fax: (905) 678-0774

Canadian Sanitation Supply Association
300 Mill Road, Suite G-10
Etobicoke, ON M9C 4W7
Telephone: (416) 620-9320
Fax: (416) 620-7199
E-mail: info@cssa.com

Japan Automobile Manufacturers Association Canada
151 Bloor Street West, Suite 460
Toronto, ON M5S 1S4
Telephone: (416) 968-0150
Fax: (416) 968-7095
Web site: JAMA@jama.ca

Machinery and Equipment Manufacturers' Association of Canada
116 Albert Street, Suite 701
Ottawa, ON K1P 5G3
Telephone: (613) 232-7213
Fax: (613) 232-7381

Nonprescription Drug Manufacturers Association of Canada
1111 Prince of Wales Drive, Suite 406
Ottawa, ON K2C 3T2
Telephone: (613) 723-0777
Fax.: (613) 723-0779
E-mail: ndmac@ndmac.ca

Petroleum Services Association of Canada
540–5th Avenue S.W., Suite 1800
Calgary, AB T2P 0M2
Telephone: (403) 264-4195
Fax: (403) 263-7174

Canadian Sphagnum Peat Moss Association
4 Wycliff Place
St. Albert, AB T8N 3Y8
Telephone: (403) 460-8280
Fax: (403) 459-0939

Appendix E
THE CARNET

A carnet is a customs document that allows you to export goods temporarily to another country, and re-export them back into Canada, without going through extensive customs procedures or paying duty. If you plan to show samples, or demonstrate equipment, or leave equipment for a short time, in a country other than the United States or Mexico, you should obtain a carnet. (For the United States and Mexico, you do not need a carnet because of the NAFTA.) You get the carnet from the Canadian Chamber of Commerce, well in advance of your trip.

The carnet system was developed by the International Bureau of Chambers of Commerce in Paris. At the time of writing, the carnet is in use by these countries.

- Algeria
- Andorra
- Australia
- Austria
- Belgium
- Bulgaria
- Canada
- China
- Croatia
- Cyprus

- ◆ Czech Republic
- ◆ Estonia
- ◆ France
- ◆ Gibraltar
- ◆ Hong Kong (China)
- ◆ Iceland
- ◆ Israel
- ◆ Ivory Coast
- ◆ Korea (South)
- ◆ Luxembourg
- ◆ Malaysia
- ◆ Mauritius
- ◆ Netherlands
- ◆ Norway
- ◆ Portugal
- ◆ Senegal
- ◆ Slovak Republic
- ◆ South Africa
- ◆ Sri Lanka
- ◆ Switzerland
- ◆ Tunisia
- ◆ United Kingdom
- ◆ Denmark
- ◆ Finland
- ◆ Germany
- ◆ Greece
- ◆ Hungary
- ◆ India
- ◆ Italy
- ◆ Japan
- ◆ Lebanon
- ◆ Macedonia
- ◆ Malta
- ◆ Morocco
- ◆ New Zealand
- ◆ Poland
- ◆ Romania
- ◆ Singapore
- ◆ Slovenia
- ◆ Spain
- ◆ Sweden
- ◆ Thailand
- ◆ Turkey
- ◆ United States of America

The carnet document consists of a folder with a space for a list of products you want to include under the carnet and a series of colour-coded vouchers. There are two vouchers for each country you enter and depart from, including Canada. Each voucher serves as a customs document and is detached by the customs official processing your carnet shipment when you leave Canada, when you enter your country of destination, when you leave that country, and when you re-enter Canada. The entry voucher and the exit voucher taken by the customs officials are matched to show that the goods have both entered and left the country, or in the case of Canada, have left and returned.

Carnets are valid for one year from the date of issue and can be used for any number of trips during that time. They cover a wide variety of commercial samples, including jewellery, electronic products, heavy-duty equipment, and aircraft. They do not cover consumable goods or other disposable products. They are not accepted for goods exported or imported by mail.

With the carnet you do not have to fill out customs forms or pay any duties each time you enter a country with your temporary goods. You pay a single fee for the document when you apply for it, plus some form of security (certified cheque, insurance bond, or cash) equalling 40 percent of the total value of the goods listed on the carnet. This is refunded to you when you return the carnet to the Chamber of Commerce office you purchased it from and present proof that the goods have been returned to Canada.

The carnet is a very handy system for the international businessperson. Here are some practical considerations when using a carnet.

1. To validate the carnet before use, you have to take all of the equipment listed on it to the Canada Customs and Revenue Agency and have them check serial numbers against the list on the carnet. The best way to do this is when you are making your first trip with the carnet. Go to the customs office a little earlier and have them complete the validation procedure, as well as clear you for your trip.

2. Ensure that the names of all possible people who may be using the carnet are listed on it. Do not limit the list to people in your company; include people such as your agent, if he might have to travel with the equipment.

3. If you are travelling with the carnet and equipment, plan your trip so that you arrive at the departure airport during the hours of operation of the customs office. If your flight is at eight in the morning and the office does not open until then, you will have a problem.

4. Try to limit the number of containers in which your carnet equipment or samples are packed. If you have several containers, and one gets lost en route, the customs people will probably not clear your carnet until you have found the missing items. Many trade show participants have had to do without their demonstrations because customs held up an incomplete shipment.

GLOSSARY

ADVISING BANK

A Canadian bank that provides you, as the exporter, with the terms and conditions of the letter of credit your buyer has arranged in order to pay you.

AGENT

An individual or company retained by an exporter to represent a particular line of goods to buyers in a specified region of country.

AIR WAYBILL

This document is provided by an airline to the exporter when the goods are turned over for shipment. It confirms that a shipment has been accepted, but it does not specify on which flight the shipment will be sent, nor exactly when it will arrive at its destination.

AREA CONTROL LIST

A Canadian government list of countries for which an export permit is required. The countries on the list are usually those on which sanctions have been imposed by organizations such as the United Nations. The reasons can vary from such matters as human rights violations to supporting international terrorism.

BACK-TO-BACK FINANCING

The practice of using the same currency throughout a transaction, thus reducing the risk of currency fluctuation.

BARE BOAT CHARTER

A boat that is chartered for freighting purposes, with the chartering party providing its own crew and supplies.

BILL OF LADING

The contract of carriage between a shipper and a shipping company, with full contract details usually printed on the back of the document. The bill of lading was originally developed for use in ocean shipping, but has since been adapted for other forms of shipping, including the truck bill of lading, the rail bill of lading, and the air bill of lading or air waybill.

C&F

Cost and freight, an internationally recognized shipping term (Incoterm). It is used when a buyer requests a quotation on the cost of the goods and freight to the port of destination, but not the insurance. Usually employed by purchasers who have a blanket insurance policy for all their shipping.

C&I

Cost and insurance, an internationally recognized shipping term (Incoterm). It is used when a buyer requests a quotation on the cost of the goods and insurance to the port of destination, but not the freight. Usually employed by purchasers who have a contract with a shipping company for all their shipping.

CARIBCAN

Commonwealth Caribbean countries tariff treatment that applies to imports from commonwealth Caribbean countries.

CARNET

A Customs document that allows you to export goods temporarily to another country, and re-import them into Canada, without going through extensive Customs procedures or paying duty.

CFS-CFS

Container freight station to container freight station. The term implies a shipment packaged by a freight forwarder with other shipments in a container; when the container arrives at the forwarder's warehouse in the foreign destination, the forwarder's representative destuffs the container and contacts the buyer.

CFS-CY

Container freight station to container yard. The term is for a shipment packaged by a freight forwarder with other shipments in a container; when the container arrives at the foreign destination the buyer picks it up and destuffs it. The buyer then returns the container to the forwarder.

CIF

Cost, insurance, and freight, an internationally recognized shipping term (Incoterm). It is used when a buyer requests a quotation on the cost of the goods, the freight, and insurance to the port of destination. It is usually followed by a reference to the shipment's port of destination. For example, CIF YVR is cost, insurance, and freight to Vancouver.

CONFIRMING HOUSE

A Canadian-based agent for a foreign buyer, empowered to make and confirm orders on behalf of its overseas clients. The confirming house guarantees to pay you, eliminating any credit risk, and may also arrange financing for the buyer.

COPYRIGHT

Copyrights are for literary, artistic, dramatic, or musical works, as well as software. When you create an original work in Canada you automatically have copyright protection. This also applies to citizens of countries who are signatories to the Berne Convention or the Universal Copyright Convention, or a country that is a member of the World Trade Organization. The copyright usually lasts for 50 years after the death of the author, except for photographs, cinematographs, and sound recordings, which are covered for 50 years after they were created.

CUSTOMS BROKER

A person or company that processes goods through the customs authority of their country on behalf of private individuals and commercial enterprises engaged in importing.

CY-CFS

Container yard to container freight station. The term for a shipment packaged by the exporter and delivered to the carrier's terminal. When the container arrives at the foreign destination, a representative of the carrier destuffs it and contacts the buyer.

CY-CY

Container yard to container yard. The term for a shipment packaged by the exporter and delivered to the carrier's terminal. When the container arrives at the foreign destination the buyer picks it up and destuffs it, then returns the container to the shipper.

D/A

Documents against acceptance. A term draft for payment of goods being shipped. The buyer receives the goods and accepts the draft, agreeing to pay you for them within a set period.

D/P

Documents against payment. A sight draft for payment of goods being shipped. The buyer is required to pay for the goods before receiving any documentation on them.

DESTUFF

To unpack a container.

DISTRIBUTOR

Buys goods from an exporter and resells them in the local market, usually on the terms and at the price the distributor determines.

DUMPING

The purchase and importation of goods into a country at lower prices than they would earn in their own domestic market.

EXCHANGE RATE

The price of one currency in terms of another.

EXPORT CONTROL LIST

A Canadian government list of goods that require an export permit. The goods include items such as munitions, nuclear-related goods, and chemicals that could be used in the production of illicit drugs.

ExW

Ex Warehouse or Ex Work, an internationally recognized shipping term (Incoterm). It is used when a buyer wants a quotation on the price of goods at their point of origin, and nothing else.

FACTORING

The practice of purchasing foreign receivables from exporters for immediate cash, then collecting the debt from the buyers.

FAS

Free along side, an internationally recognized shipping term (Incoterm). It is used when a buyer requests a quotation on the cost of the goods to their point of export and through customs formalities. All other costs become the responsibility of the purchaser.

FOB

Free on board, an internationally recognized shipping term (Incoterm). It is used when a buyer requests a quotation on the cost of the goods plus the cost (including loading charges) of putting them on a vessel or aircraft. The exporter must take the goods through Canadian customs.

FORFAITING

Your bank or forfaiter purchases the promissory notes your buyer has provided to you, then forwards the full amount to you, less a discount charge.

FREIGHT FORWARDER

A person or company that handles the shipment of goods. The responsibilities of a freight forwarder include arranging all shipment details and completing the documentation.

FTA

Canada-United States Free Trade Agreement implemented on January 1, 1989, and replaced by the North American Free Trade Agreement (NAFTA) on January 1, 1994.

GATT

General Agreement on Tariff and Trade created at the end of the Second World War and adopted by the leading trading nations at the time.

HS

The Harmonized Commodity Description and Coding System, used by the United States, Canada, and Mexico to describe goods. It is used to identify tariffs that apply to the goods, for freight documentation, and for reporting trade statistics between the countries. You can get the HS number for your products by contacting your nearest Canada Customs and Revenue Agency office.

IATA

International Aeronautics Transport Association, which represents not only the airline carriers, but the many freight forwarders that also belong to the organization.

INCOTERMS

Rules established by the International Chamber of Commerce to standardize the use of international trade terms. Incoterms determine the division of cost and risk between the buyer and seller, and the obligation each has to the other under the contract.

INDUSTRIAL DESIGNS

Industrial designs are for the shape, pattern or ornamentation applied to an industrially produced object. There are no reciprocal agreements between Canada and other countries for the protection of industrial designs.

INTERMODAL or MULTIMODAL TRANSPORT

The use of more than one type of transport during the course of a single shipment.

LA MORDIDA

Derived from the Mexican word for "bite," la mordida refers to the Mexican practice of bribing those in positions of authority to perform certain functions, provide favours, and so on. It is less prevalent today than it once was in Mexico, as the government and the private sector unite to combat the practice.

LETTER OF CREDIT

A written undertaking for payment to a supplier made by a bank at the request of a buyer. Letters of credit are also called documentary credits, because they rely on the provision of documents by the seller for confirmation that all conditions to a sale have been met. Such documents might include a bill of lading, an inspection certificate, a certificate of origin, and the like.

LINER SERVICES

The regularly scheduled services available through steamship lines on established trade routes.

LTL

A truck shipping term that refers to a less than full truck load.

MAQUILADORAS

Derived from the Mexican term "maguila." The portion of grain a miller keeps in return for grinding it. Maquiladoras are manufacturing and assembly plants, originally established along the Mexican-US border to accommodate American needs for cheap labour and to stimulate the Mexican economy by providing jobs, training, and manufacturing equipment to Mexican workers. Today there are thousand of maquiladoras in operation throughout Mexico.

MFN TARIFF TREATMENT

Most Favoured Nation Tariff Treatment. It applies to the goods of all countries with which Canada has a trading agreement.

MT TARIFF TREATMENT

Mexico Tariff Treatment initiated under NAFTA.

MUST TARIFF TREATMENT

Mexico-US Tariff Treatment initiated under NAFTA.

NAFTA

North American Free Trade Agreement, among Canada, the United States, and Mexico, implemented on January 1, 1994. The major benefit of NAFTA is the elimination of tariffs between the three countries. Additional benefits include allowance of cross-border trade in services; liberalization of transportation services; and better access for professionals such as engineers.

NEGOTIATING BANK

The Canadian bank that cashes the letter of credit provided by the buyer's bank, after you have met all of the conditions stated in the letter.

NICHE MARKETING

Identifying a specific market for your product and focusing on the needs of that market, rather than trying to sell to a broader constituency. Niche marketing has become increasingly popular in the complex domestic markets of the western world, and is often used by exporters trying to break into the American market.

NVO

Non-Vessel Owning carrier (NVOCC or Non-Vessel Operating Common Carrier in the United States). An ocean freight forwarder term. NVOs consolidate small shipments into containers destined for the same foreign market.

OPEN ACCOUNT

The practice of shipping goods as soon as an order is received, then invoicing the buyer for payment within a set term. This approach is common in domestic transactions, and saves the exporter some expense and paperwork, but is risky.

PATENTS

Patents are new technologies (processes, structures, and functions). The Patent Cooperation Treaty (PCT), administered by the World Intellectual Property Organization based in Geneva, assists you in filing patents in other countries. The PCT provides standardized international filing procedures, and under it you can file for a patent in up to 89 countries. This eases the pressure of the requirement to file an application in another country quickly. Instead, you can file within Canada, in English, and have up to 20 or 30 months to complete the application in other countries.

PRO FORMA INVOICE

A quotation or invitation to buy provided by the seller to the buyer. It is clearly stamped "pro forma," and becomes a formal order once the buyer has signed it.

TARIFF TREATMENT
The duty rate established under the terms of a trading agreement with another country.

TEAM TRACKS
A railway siding that is owned and operated by the railways for public use. Some companies that make extensive use of rail lines maintain their own private sidings.

TL
A shipping abbreviation that refers to a full truck load.

TRADING HOUSE
A Canadian-based export and import intermediary or broker whose chief function is to find foreign buyers for its client company products.

TRANSSHIPMENT
Shipment of goods through another country without entering the commerce of the country.

ULD
Unit Loading Device. A term applied to containers used in air shipment. The main purpose of a ULD is to consolidate general cargo into units that are easier to handle and can be secured during shipment.

UST
United States Tariff treatment. It was first established under the FTA, and is continued under NAFTA.

OTHER TITLES IN THE
SELF-COUNSEL BUSINESS SERIES

MARKETING YOUR SERVICE

Jean Withers and Carol Vipperman

$24.95 CAN

1-55180-395-X

Service businesses today face stiff competition. Nine out of ten new businesses are in the service sector. Accountants and lawyers, hairstylists and health-club owners alike need to understand the distinctive nature of marketing a service, and each must devise a custom-made strategy to succeed. This book explains how to develop a marketing plan that will work for your service business. This new edition, which includes a CD-ROM, will help you —

- Plan for business success
- Learn the keys to dynamic service marketing
- Position your service business
- Implement your marketing action plan

MARKETING YOUR PRODUCT

Donald Cyr and Douglas Gray

$24.95 CAN

1-55180-394-1

This marketing book is for the real world, not just the classroom. An informative planning guide that covers all the essentials, this newly updated and expanded edition demonstrates how to carve a niche for any product in today's competitive, fast-paced, and often fickle consumer environment.

Now including a chapter on the value of the Internet as a marketing tool, this long-trusted guide clearly explains common theories and provides step-by-step advice using plenty of helpful worksheets. This new edition, which includes a CD-ROM, helps you —

- Plan for business success
- Get updated information on the Internet
- Develop the competitive edge
- Understand your customers

WIN THE GREEN CARD LOTTERY!

Marybeth Rael and J. Stephen Wilson

$12.95 CAN

1-55180-397-6

Win The Green Card Lottery! is written for those who wish to immigrate to the United States. Whether you are an international student already living in the US or Canada, a visitor present temporarily on a tourist visa, or a tradesman or professional living in a foreign country, this inexpensive book collects together everything you need to know to apply for the DV-2004 green card (diversity visa) lottery.

As a complete "do-it-yourself" information kit, this guide covers the entire process from entering the lottery to obtaining your green card. It will show you the correct way to apply for the visa lottery (with no expensive "application fees") and is written by insiders who have won. Furthermore, by registering for the lottery yourself, you are assured your application is actually mailed in.

Win the Green Card Lottery! provides previously unpublished tips designed to increase your chances of winning. If you read this book and follow the instructions, the authors estimate that you can almost triple your chances of winning a green card, depending on your specific country of birth.

Order Form

All prices are subject to change without notice. Books are available in book, department, and stationery stores. If you cannot buy the book through a store, please use this order form.

(*Please print.*)

Name _____

Address _____

Charge to: ❏ Visa   ❏ MasterCard

Account number: _____

Validation Date: _____

Expiry date: _____

Signature: _____

YES, please send me:

_____ *Marketing Your Service*

_____ *Marketing Your Product*

_____ *Win the Green Card Lottery!*

Please add $4.00 for postage and handling.

Please add 7% GST to your order.

❏ Check here for a free catalog.

Please send your order to the nearest location:

Self-Counsel Press
1481 Charlotte Road
North Vancouver, BC, V7J 1H1

Self-Counsel Press
4 Bram Court
Brampton, ON, L6W 3R6

Visit our Internet Web Site at:
www.self-counsel.com